THE WILL TO WALK

LEI DIANSHENG

ACA PUBLISHING LTD

Published by
ACA Publishing Ltd.
University House
11-13 Lower Grosvenor Place,
London SW1W 0EX, UK
Tel: +44 20 3289 3885
E-mail: info@alaincharlesasia.com
Web: www.alaincharlesasia.com

Beijing Office
Tel: +86 (0)10 8472 1250

Author: Lei Diansheng
Translator: Lü Yueran

Published by ACA Publishing Ltd in association with China Translation & Publishing House

Original Chinese Text © Lei Diansheng © 信念: 十年徒步中国 (*Xin Nian: Shi Nian Tu Bu Zhong Guo*) 2017, China Translation and Publishing House, Beijing, China

English Translation © 2020, ACA Publishing Ltd, London, UK

ALL RIGHTS RESERVED. NO PART OF THIS PUBLICATION MAY BE REPRODUCED IN MATERIAL FORM, BY ANY MEANS, WHETHER GRAPHIC, ELECTRONIC, MECHANICAL OR OTHER, INCLUDING PHOTOCOPYING OR INFORMATION STORAGE, IN WHOLE OR IN PART, AND MAY NOT BE USED TO PREPARE OTHER PUBLICATIONS WITHOUT WRITTEN PERMISSION FROM THE PUBLISHER.

The greatest care has been taken to ensure accuracy but the publisher can accept no responsibility for errors or omissions, or for any liability occasioned by relying on its content.

Paperback ISBN: 978-1-910760-90-1
eBook ISBN: 978-1-910760-91-8

A catalogue record for *The Will to Walk* is available from the National Bibliographic Service of the British Library.

CONTENTS

1. 1998: A Difficult Beginning Like Any Other — 1
2. 1999: Walking Cultivates the Mind — 10
3. 2000: Happiness is Simple — 39
4. 2001: Walking Enriches Life — 73
5. 2002: A Long Pilgrimage — 116
6. 2003: A Mesmerising Tale — 145
7. 2004: Homeward Journey — 160
8. 2005: My Heart, Farthest Away — 174
9. 2006: Walking to Purity — 187
10. 2007: The Last Challenge — 204
11. 2008: The Song of Life — 217
    Afterword: On the Road — 243

About the Author — 247

A DECADE-LONG JOURNEY THROUGH CHINA

My biggest dream is being able to walk across China. I spent ten years improving my physical condition, accumulating funds and improving my knowledge of the natural world. As it is finally time to lift my backpack and set out on my dream, and as my body and mind are becoming more mature and full of spirit, I feel nothing can stop me from moving forward, only death.

1998

A DIFFICULT BEGINNING LIKE ANY OTHER

———

After ten years preparation, I took the first step of my journey on the morning of 20 October 1998.

However, it was not until I finally hit the road that I realised everything wasn't as simple as I had imagined…

National Highway 102, the first kilometre

As I departed the inn, my third oldest brother and a few friends came to say goodbye. I handed over my favourite shaver to my brother and said to him: "Don't throw it away, even if it breaks. If I don't come back, please keep it as a memento."

I almost couldn't hold back the tears as I was talking. My brother went silent for a moment, and said solemnly: "Little brother, come home safely!"

At 8.20am, I bade farewell to my family and friends by the zero kilometre sign of National Highway 102 in Harbin, Heilongjiang. I finally took the first step of the journey. It was 234 kilometres to Changchun, and 1,303 kilometres to Beijing.

Those numbers on the large sign above me appeared almost surreal. As I stared at them, I understood more and more that I would be using my own two feet to achieve those numbers. I looked up at the blue, cloudless sky and thought: What pleasant autumn weather! Does such an auspicious day mean that I will enjoy safe travel? Does it mean I will achieve my dream? Does it mean I can turn calamities into blessings?

Everything was unknown; everything was filled with infinite potential.

The local press came to interview me after they heard about my journey. I was wearing a bright red coat and a baseball cap. The red banner on my backpack stood out prominently. It read: 'A Cross-Century Journey Across China – Lei Diansheng'.

Although the 48kg backpack made my shoulders feel a little uncomfortable, I knew I couldn't delay any further. Therefore, after a few words with the TV and newspaper reporters, I tightened my shoulder straps and waved to my family, friends and the journalists, exclaiming: "I'll see you in ten years!"

Then, I went past the crowd without looking back.

I had taken only a few steps when I heard a reporter ask my brother: "Why is your brother taking this trip? Does he have any mental issues?"

"He doesn't. There's nothing wrong with him," my brother replied, offended by the question.

Waving goodbye before departure

I could feel the crowd looking at me with a mix of curiosity, disdain and even resentfulness. Despite my best efforts to ignore them, I still felt hurt. Having taken just a few steps, I had already become disheartened. Tears started to well up, but I managed to hold them back. I looked up at the cloudless blue sky to remind myself once more why I was doing this. The sky was so clear and bright that day, as if it had been washed clean of imperfections.

Meanwhile, I heard another person shout out: "Lei Diansheng, even if you just walk to Shuangcheng [a satellite city just fifty kilometres from Harbin] and come back, it will still count as walking across China, just that you didn't finish the trip. Don't be so stupid as to really walk for ten years!"

It was no use answering. At this moment, explaining myself wouldn't be easy. I resolved to stop thinking and just started walking. What was important was to take the first step, a step I had been wanting to take for a decade.

An arrow fired cannot return to the bow

That afternoon, I arrived in the village of Baojiawobao in Shuangcheng, Harbin, after walking along National Highway 102. According to my original plan, I should have continued walking until Happy Village, which was further down the road. Unfortunately, my feet hurt so much from blisters that I decided to rest there before setting off once more.

Mr He, the village head, met me and insisted that I stay at his home to rest. Prior to going to bed, I used a needle to burst the blisters on my feet, squeezing out the blood and pus, and putting ointment on the wound. I had a sleepless night from the burning pain.

I soon realised that not everything would be as easy as I originally imagined. My feet were already battered after just one day. Could I really overcome all the difficulties that lay ahead? At that moment, I recalled the saying: 'The beginning is always the hardest.' I silently vowed to myself: Lei Diansheng, you must overcome the hardships and persist to the end.

Early next morning, I got up from bed feeling a sharp pain. At first, I had to hold myself up against the wall in order to walk, trying to reduce the pressure of my feet touching the ground. After practising for a while, I managed to hit the road again.

A few kind-hearted drivers pulled over as they saw me limping, asking whether I needed a lift. I declined with thanks. Seeing my determination to keep walking, some passers-by shouted: "You can do it!" That gave me a sense of pride.

Initially I could handle the weight of my backpack. But the further I walked, the more I realised that it was starting to affect my speed. So I called my nephew Chunming and asked him to take the bus to Happy Village to bring back those items I did not need.

He was already waiting for me in the village when I arrived. I was afraid that my family had become worried about me, so I tried to hide the pain on my face. I was covered in sweat from the discomfort as I walked towards the post office to get stamps. I had to sit on the ground afterwards to burst the blood blisters on my feet with a small knife and spray alcohol on them to prevent infection.

Chunming saw me as I was treating the wounds, and he held me as he said: "Uncle, please come home with me. This is too hard to watch."

He dragged my backpack towards him as he was saying this. I stopped him: "I have already left home. I can't go back now."

I persuaded him to go home at once. As we were saying goodbye, I instructed him not to tell the family about my ailments. He nodded and left reluctantly with tears in his eyes.

At about noon, I arrived in Shuangcheng District. Due to my sore feet, I had no choice but to stay there overnight. Taking off my shoes, I discovered that I could wring out blood from the insoles. My ankle started to hurt too. I made the calculation that I had only walked twenty-two kilometres during the day, far less than what I had planned.

As soon as I entered the city, someone called out: "Hey! Aren't you Lei Diansheng? We read about you in the news. We admire what you're doing. Can I have your autograph?" Receiving such recognition from strangers after only two days of the trip, I felt moved and greatly encouraged.

As more and more people saw my limping state, they all urged me to stay put until I was fully recovered. I appreciated the advice, but I knew if I rested now I wouldn't be able to face bigger challenges ahead. Hence, I decided to continue the trip the next day.

After a few more days, I gradually got used to walking long distances. Even though my feet had still not fully recovered, I was able to increase my speed from twenty kilometres a day to sometimes close to forty kilometres a day.

I pushed myself as far as I could over the first two weeks. I walked along the ice-covered Lalin and Songhua rivers, the bitter cold blizzards of Jilin, and finally into Liaoning.

Unfortunately, a few more blisters appeared on my feet. Once, I was piercing my blisters on the side of the road when an old man came along. He stopped his cart and inquired whether I had scissors. I nodded and hurriedly handed a pair to him. He went behind his horse, cut off a clump of hair from its tail and gave it to me.

"Use alcohol to sterilise the hair and thread the needle with it," he instructed. "Soak your feet in hot water before you go to sleep in order to relax and clean your feet. Then, if you thread the needle through the blister and leave the horsehair inside, you'll feel much better when you pull it out the next day."

Dubiously, I put the horsehair in my backpack. "Also," he continued, "wear two layers of socks when you walk. I did this myself a long time ago and rarely had blisters after walking dozens of kilometres."

The old man offered to give me a ride but I refused with thanks. Later, when I tried his method to treat the blisters, it actually worked. What a pleasant surprise!

1999

WALKING CULTIVATES THE MIND

———

Abbot Wanfeng once said to me: "*Walking is like practising Buddhism.*"

What is happiness? I asked myself.

I realised, at this moment, that happiness was a bottle of out-of-date beer, two packs of instant noodles, a jar of pickles and a can of fish.

A narrow escape from death

In January 1999, I managed to cross into Linfen, Shanxi Province. The most famous scenic spot in the area is the Yellow River's Hukou Waterfall, located in Jinxian Hukou Village.

The ground on both sides of the river was frozen. Few people travel here in winter. Even from a distance of three kilometres, a thunderous noise could be heard, giving a sense of the waterfall's magnificence. As I approached the waterfall, the air became more humid. As the sound got louder and louder and the mountains became more prominent, the waterfall gradually came into view. The Yellow River water was cascading down the cliff wall with tremendous force.

I walked up to the waterfall, gasping at the spectacular view in front of me. It was as if the entire Yellow River was falling into a giant teapot. The rocks on both sides of the river formed a narrow outlet, funnelling water down a river that was previously hundreds of metres wide into a gap of just tens of metres. The accumulation of downstream energy powered the force of the water down the cliff. The sound deafened everything around it.

The river sits in a valley of mountains. The rocks at the bottom of the waterfall formed deep crevices from the constant impact of the water. The rapids rushed down so strongly that it looked as if white stallions were galloping towards the bottom of the valley. This was the charm of the Hukou Waterfall.

Due to the low temperature, thick ice had formed on the surface of the water that buffeted the surrounding rocks. Under bright sunlight, the ice shined liked a smooth and dazzling mirror. The huge waves created by the enormous current painted a colourful halo under the sun, like a rainbow after rain.

I was overwhelmed by the view. As I kept on pressing down the camera shutter to capture the image, I suddenly slipped and began to tumble down the rocks. My heart tightened. Soon I was going to fall into the river valley, and in the midst of struggling I saw a faint glimmer of hope in the form of a small cavity. I stretched out my foot in the hope of arresting my fall, and at last I stopped my body from sliding down further. All those years of training had proved their worth.

Hugging the ice wall with the utmost caution, I coordinated my limbs to slowly crawl up. Five minutes passed and I had only been able to move about four metres. Time seemed to have frozen. My heart raced so much that it felt like it was jumping out of my throat. Even after managing to crawl back up and leave this dangerous area, my heart was still pounding from what had just happened. My body, covered with sweat, shivered with fear and exhaustion. Relieved at arriving at a place of safety, I dropped to the ground.

The spectacular Hukou Waterfall

Later, I learned from locals that no one could survive a fall down the valley. They told me that it had happened to a man previously and his body was found several kilometres downstream. I was traumatised by the incident.

It was 10 January when I left Hukou and continued my journey. I had experienced my first near-death encounter; I promised myself that safety must come first from now on. I would be sure to plan the next day's trip meticulously and try to predict the various kinds of danger that I may encounter.

The 'benefit' of sanitary towels

In April, I crossed the border into Jiangsu Province, having passed through Henan and Anhui.

At that time of the year, regions south of the Yangtze River are at their most beautiful. The rivers and canals form an intricate web and fresh seedlings are abundant, showing an expanse of green, in contrast to the loess plateau, through which the Yellow River runs.

While enjoying the delights of spring, I started to feel a heaviness and physical exhaustion. Having walked under the scorching sun for days on end, my clothes were soaked from my sweat and the humid weather.

My inner thighs were chafed, turning my skin purple, almost like pork liver. My soaked clothes only exacerbated the situation. The area got worse and worse and eventually became inflamed. Despite taking anti-inflammatory drugs, the condition would not improve. Every step I took was excruciatingly painful.

I had to stop walking every now and then to find a place where no one was around in order to take off my trousers, clean the wound and put on medication. A little while later I had an idea: apply anti-inflammatory medication directly onto napkins, place them over the wound and fasten them with rubber bands. However, the napkins became soaked in sweat and disintegrated in no time.

As I was passing a village store, the idea suddenly came to me of using sanitary towels to dress my wounds. People gave me strange looks when I was paying at the counter: what was this unkempt man doing here, buying sanitary towels? Is he some kind of pervert?

I saw contempt and confusion in their eyes. The shopkeeper looked at me curiously too, and finally he could not resist asking: "What do you want these for?" I told him that I needed them for the wound on my thighs. He laughed after learning the truth, but I could still hear them whisper as I walked out of the store.

The pads proved to be very effective. They were easy to fix, stayed relatively dry and did not rub my skin further. Before long, the wound healed.

On 6 April I arrived in Horse Town in Jiangyin. There, I visited the grave and former residence of Xu Xiake, whom I had admired for a long time.

Paying my respects to the ancestors, I walked around the cemetery a few times, carefully comprehending Xu Xiake's extraordinary courage and wisdom. Time seemed to wind back four hundred years. The various scenes depicted in Xu Xiake's travel journals were like films appearing before my eyes.

Xu Yesheng, a descendant of Xu Xiake

His footprints were left on famous Chinese mountains and alongside countless rivers, and his travel journals are still being published and read at home and abroad. Xu Xiake is a source of pride to the Chinese people.

At Xu Xiake's former home, his descendant Xu Yesheng welcomed me in. When he learned that I planned to walk across China, he wished me a safe journey and said he hoped my dream could come true.

Night and day

On the morning of 7 April, soon after leaving Horse Town, I came across a few people from a company called Chunyan Airline Tableware. They warmly invited me over to discuss the trip and hear my future travel plans. They showed their support by giving me a lot of good advice regarding travelling in Jiangsu.

Before long, I continued my trip south. When I was approaching Yanqiao Town, Xishan City, a car came to a halt in front of me, and out came a tall, middle-aged man. After a short conversation, I learned that he was a teacher from the Bridge engineering department of Tongji University. His name was Yang Jian.

After learning about my travel plans, he took out five hundred yuan and told me to accept it. I declined. However, he insisted: "I want to give you the money not because I take pity on you. Rather, I really hope you can make it to the end. You've only been walking for six months. There is still a long way to go. I look forward to hearing about your success."

Throughout the trip, I was moved by the generosity of strangers. I received all kinds of gifts, including bottles of water, camera film and tens and hundreds of renminbi. Most people refused to give me their names or contact details, making it impossible for me to return the favour. Therefore, what I felt from Mr Yang's words was not just kindness, but also motivation. The spiritual strength he gave me was empowering and encouraged me to keep going.

However, there was not always support and understanding.

Later, on my way to Wujiang, two young cyclists joined me. We talked as we walked along.

"Who asked you to walk across China?" one of the men asked. "How much are you getting for this?"

"Nothing. I'm doing this out of my own will, not for money."

"Don't lie. Nobody would do hard work without wanting to get paid," the other man said.

"I'm not lying," I went on. "I funded the trip myself. This is my dream."

"Dream? Doesn't everyone dream of money?"

"Yes, except a dead person or an idiot!"

I was speechless, yet they still chattered nonstop about money. Seeing that I would not be drawn, they gave me one last piece of advice: "Don't be so stupid. You should go home. If you don't, there'll be no one to take care of you if you die on the road."

Satisfied, they rode away without looking back.

Seeing them fade into the distance, my heart sank.

My mood had been upbeat and full of admiration for this beautiful land south of the Yangtze. This area was much wealthier than my home town and I could feel the long history and deep culture from the friendly people. However, the two cyclists who supposedly represented the future of our country demonstrated the narrowness of mind of those fixated with money.

Walking, a way to practise Buddhism

Accompanied by a slight drizzle, I arrived in Anqing, Anhui Province on 3 May. The first place I wanted to visit was the Yingjiang Temple along the Yangtze River.

The temple was founded in the seventh year of Emperor Taizu's rule during the Song dynasty (AD 974). During the Ming and the Qing dynasties, the temple was repeatedly rebuilt, and it wasn't constructed on a larger scale until the early Qing dynasty. Unfortunately, the temple burned to ashes during the eleventh year of Emperor Xianfeng's governance during the Qing (1861); and it was rebuilt again in the first year of Emperor Tongzhi's reign (1862).

The collection of Buddhist sutras at the temple contained tens of thousands of Confucian classics and in history had produced many eminent monks. It was a place of great spiritual influence. I devoutly visited many temples on my journey and was lucky enough to get to know some monks. The experience greatly helped me maintain a calm and persevering outlook. Whenever I walked into a temple, I felt my mind and soul become refreshed and strengthened.

I took a stick of incense by the temple gate, lit it and then inserted it into the incense burner. With my hands clasped together, I kneeled to worship Buddha. Strolling across the temple, I passed the Hall of

Heavenly King and the Mahavira Hall, and then observed what is known as 'the first Yangtze River tower', the Zhenfeng Pagoda.

This seven-storey octagonal pagoda made of brick was built in the Ming dynasty, experiencing more than 400 years of history. It has stood quietly like an old man, silently witnessing all that was happening in the world. Through the ages, the pagoda endured violence and destruction, yet managed to survive. Those walking towards the pagoda can feel a sense of calmness and serenity touching their souls, a testament to the pagoda's strength through time itself. In this sense, the pagoda is similar to those people who manage to make it through tough times and are able to reach peace and enlightenment.

For the entire afternoon, I walked around the area, hoping my heart would become attuned to the serenity and ancient charm of this place. When it was close to dusk, I went seeking temporary lodging at the temple's welcome centre. A benevolent old man came forward and said: "You look tired from travel. I presume you've come from afar."

I briefly introduced myself and asked him whether I could stay overnight. He nodded with a smile: "You must have gone through a lot of hardships along the way. Abbot Wanfeng is a senior monk at this temple. I can introduce you to him."

Soon, Senior Abbot Wanfeng and Abbot Huizhen received me. Abbot Wanfeng was already eighty-six years old, and from the moment I first saw him, his thin face and clear, deep eyes left a lasting impression.

Abbot Wanfeng became a monk when he was very young. Wishing to perform good deeds, he founded an organisation during the Anti-Japanese War to rescue orphans. In order to build the Yingjiang Temple into a formal monastery and repair the Zhenfeng Pagoda, he worked through sickness and health to raise funds. Due to his devotion, the monastery became what it is today.

Both abbots were surprised to hear my story. Abbot Wanfeng asked me with concern: "What has been the biggest difficulty during your trip?"

I told him I was not afraid of arduous conditions; however, I could not bear failing to be understood, having to suffer verbal irony, sarcasm and even gratuitous maltreatment.

Abbot Wanfeng went silent for a moment and said: "Walking is like practising Buddhism."

Abbot Wanfeng and me

I could not fully decipher what he said, but it would not have been wise for me to inquire further. Therefore, I just nodded and said that I would try to overcome my distracting thoughts and focus on walking with all my devotion.

As I prepared to say goodbye, Abbot Wanfeng suddenly gestured to me. With trembling hands, he took out a small, ancient cloth pouch. Peeling open layers of the cloth, a neat stack of small notes was revealed. Abbot Wanfeng drew two hundred yuan and handed it to me, saying: "My child, this is not much, but please keep it. You still have a long way to go. Remember, you should leave early and rest early every day. You must take care of your health. Amituofo!"

At first, I refused to accept the money, but I was forced to relent due to his persistence. Feeling very grateful, I bowed deeply to Abbot Wanfeng with my palms together.

Throughout the night, his exhortation echoed in my mind. I became cautious during many crucial moments upon remembering his words:

"Walking is like practising Buddhism." Another of his sayings, "leave early and rest early", went on to form part of my walking strategy in later years.

After morning class at the temple the next day, I bade farewell to Abbot Wanfeng and continued on. I would later find out that this was the last time I would see him.

In June 2002, when I was in Tibet, I heard that Abbot Wanfeng had passed away the previous month. The impermanence of life struck me with a sense of grief. I was told his final words were: "Life is short; one must not waste time. One must also not be greedy in this monetary society."

I kneeled silently, bowed and touched my head to the ground three times in the direction of Anqing to worship him.

'Chivalrous' robbers

With Abbot Wanfeng's blessings, I left Anqing and headed west.

On the afternoon of 5 May, I found myself in a wilderness between the counties of Huaining and Qianshan, Anhui Province.

My feet were hurting from the loose stones on the road that was flanked on both sides by towering mountain peaks. Suddenly, the sound of motorcycles could be heard from behind. I had a strong feeling of imminent danger, perhaps a robbery.

I tried to calm myself down and looked back. Emerging from the dust were two motorcycles speeding towards me. When they got closer, I saw four strong young men.

I retreated a few steps.

The motorcycles screeched to a halt roughly two metres in front of me. The four men jumped off and one man with a moustache said harshly: "Hey, we need some money. Give us your money and everything of value now!"

Pressed against the base of a cliff, I said coldly: "Hey friend, I'm just walking with a few hundred yuan on me. If you insist, I can give it to you. But I have to keep the old camera."

I watched their reaction while I was talking. Seeing that they did not intend to jump onto me, I went on: "Friend, can you let me continue my trip?"

"What are you doing?" one of them asked.

"I am backpacking across China."

"Where are you from?"

"Heilongjiang."

"How long have you been walking?"

"My goal is to walk for ten years. I have not yet completed one year."

"Who paid for your trip?"

"I support myself."

When they heard that I planned to walk for ten years, one of the men tried to persuade his companions to let me go because I seemed to have a difficult life. Taking advantage of the situation, I quickly greeted them with folded hands in front of my chest: "Thank you friends."

Then I turned and left as fast as I could.

It looked like they went blank for a moment and stopped following me. As I increased my pace, I heard the sound of engines starting. Looking back, I saw them getting on their motorcycles and swiftly driving away.

I felt very lucky. The money I carried was enough to support me for a month. I was even more worried about my camera. Even though it wasn't worth much, the precious pictures I had taken along the way made it feel like an old friend. With my skills, I might well have come out on top if we started to fight; but I couldn't risk it. Any injury sustained to myself or to them would have greatly affected my plans.

Less than thirty minutes had passed when the sound of motorcycles came again from behind. They must have changed their minds. They still wanted my money.

I unzipped my bag as fast as I could and steadily held the long knife I had brought for self-defence. If they wanted my money I would just give it to them. The highest priority was ensuring that I could get away safely.

Sure enough, it was the same motorcycles and the same people. This time they halted roughly four or five metres away from me. One of the men jumped from the bike and said to me in a loud voice: "Hey buddy, don't be so stressed out! We're here to give you some food and water."

I was astonished. Are these robbers now friends?

He approached me with a plastic bag in his hand. In the meantime, another of the men shouted: "You're a real man. My buddies and I all respect what you are doing, and we'd like to become friends."

I responded with a nod. As the man passed me the plastic bag, I peeked inside and saw two bottles of water and two boxes of crackers. It was easy to tell that the food had long expired. However, in remote mountain areas like this, selling expired food was not uncommon. I frequently bought out-of-date food during my trip. They told me that it was getting dark. Since I was still far away from the village ahead, they decided to bring me some food so I could have something to eat.

I accepted the bag, eyes slightly moist.

They also left me their numbers, telling me that if I encountered any trouble in the surrounding area, I should call them. In return, I gave them my sister's number and home address as an emergency contact.

I bade farewell to them again with my hands joined. After a few steps, I turned and waved back at them before I took big strides again onto the road.

The Ke family siblings

It was getting dark on 13 May when I arrived in Shuiyuan Village, Dade Town, Yangxin County, Hubei Province. I turned on the flashlight and walked towards the village, realising there was no lodging anywhere nearby. Finally, as I spotted a grocery store with its lights on, I walked in and learned that the closest place was fifteen kilometres away.

Next to the door sat a few people chatting, and they asked me what I was doing there. I told them I was a backpacker and that I wanted to find a place to stay for the night.

A teenager stood up and told me I could use his place. I then asked the price. An old man close by said to me: "Just give him ten yuan." With that, I followed him to his home. After stepping through a small door, I found it difficult to see anything under the dim light. I could tell, though, that this family didn't have many possessions.

Once inside the room, I told him: "I haven't eaten yet. Can you get me some food? I'll give you money."

He crouched into the kitchen without saying a word. Before long, he walked out, holding a bowl of porridge and some pickles. I became somewhat grouchy. I had walked the entire day, I thought, and now I'm tired and starving. I needed more food than this. Besides, I told him that I would pay.

As I was complaining to myself, three children came out from a room in the back, two girls and a boy. They looked timid.

The little boy spoke to the teenager: "Big brother, we're hungry."

"I know," the teenager replied. "Let's eat after our guest finishes."

Under the dim light, I saw that the four kids were wearing old and shabby clothes, and there was no colour in their faces. They looked at me with eyes full of doubt, curiosity and fear.

"Are they your younger siblings?" I asked the young fellow who had prepared the meal for me.

"Yes."

"Where are your parents?"

"A few years ago, our mum committed suicide by drinking pesticide after a fight with Dad."

My heart clenched. "What about your dad?"

"Dad left home after our mum died. We haven't heard from him since. He probably doesn't want us any more."

"Do you have other relatives at home?" I asked, as I tried hard to control my emotions.

"It's only us four and our grandma. Grandma is over seventy years old, and she's not in good shape. She's lying in the room now."

After listening to his words, I could feel my heart aching. Suddenly I understood that it was already awkward for the young fellow to cook a bowl of porridge for me. I couldn't eat alone, so I told the eldest brother: "Come here, let's eat together."

The young fellow was the eldest brother of the four siblings. His name was Ke Youyong and he was eighteen years old. The second eldest brother was Ke Youmeng and he was fourteen; the eldest sister, Ke Hongmei, twelve years old; the youngest sister, Ke Limei, nine years old. When their mother died and their father left home, Ke Youyong was only twelve and attending school at fourth grade. The youngest of them was merely three years old at the time. The family tragedy forced

Youyong and Youmeng to quit school to farm in order to provide food for the children and their grandma. Six years had gone by with this family in shambles, living in this dilapidated house and subsisting on their meagre wealth. Six years of living in a two-room house, being forced to suffer and wither away without the care of the other villagers.

The Ke family

That night, I was lying on a straw mattress, unable to fall asleep. The memory of my parents and the image of the four children sharing a worn-out bed made my heart clench again. They were effectively orphans, having to bear these difficulties at such an early stage in their lives. I was able to empathise with them because I had been through something similar. How could they manage to drag themselves out of poverty if they did not go to school?

I became sleepless, lost in thought. I had to do something for this unfortunate family.

Early next morning I took Youyong to the town office that was a few kilometres away. I managed to talk to a few government officials about the Ke family's situation and my thoughts on how to assist them. I planned to save money every year to pay for Youyong's sisters' education. I also expressed the hope that the government could help the children, at least with their living expenses.

In the beginning, they were intrigued by my backpacking experience; however, after they heard my petition for government subsidy, they showed concern. They told me that many poor families lived in the town. The government did not have the ability to solve all the issues, and it would be unfair to just help a single family. The root of the problem could only be resolved if we developed the economy and increased the villagers' income. What they said was undeniable, so we returned home empty-handed.

Once we got home, I handed Youyong four hundred yuan to pay for his sisters' tuition, enough for two years. I also charged him with the task of supervising their education. Suffering would only be temporary; if they applied themselves, life would get better. I promised to send more money later to help them. Since it was close to the Dragon Boat Festival, I left another twenty yuan for the family to spend for the holiday, and I also bought some medicine for the sickly grandma.

Youyong cried when I put on my backpack, ready to hit the road. I patted him and his brother on the shoulder and said to them: "Please don't cry. You two have to stay strong. You will not only need to work hard to feed the family, but also educate yourselves. If you want to change your fate, you will have to rely on your own efforts."

With the four kids insisting on escorting me, we walked together for a very long time. When we arrived at a small hillside, I told them to go home. Limei, the youngest sister, came over and pulled my sleeve.

"Uncle Lei," she said, "please live with us after you finish the trip. We will be older then and can cook a lot of food for you every day."

Those naïve words made it hard for me hold back my tears. I hurriedly turned and walked forward. At a bend in the road, I looked back and could still see their small hands waving in the air.

Walking on the mountain road, I could not help but burst into tears. Was I crying for my own misfortune when I was a child? Or for the hardships those children were going through? Or for their unpredictable future? I could not tell. Crying relieved the heaviness in my heart and turned sadness into encouragement. I had to come back and visit these helpless children.

I thought about the family throughout my trip and never forgot the promise I made. Every year I mailed them tuition fees through the post office and made phone calls to check on their progress.

When you reach out to help others, it enriches your spirit and inspires your mind. Throughout the trip, I received countless acts of care and generosity from people I did not know. That day I was able to pass on a little of my own love and care by helping a few children. I felt that kindness could grow from seeds of love.

Youyong once told me during a phone call that even though the town couldn't support them, what I left for the family was enough to fund his two sisters' education. He said that he wanted to go out to work in the city so that his sisters could continue to attend school.

For a few years, Youyong and his youngest sister kept sending me letters. I was only able to read them six years later after I arrived back home. I could tell that they had become much more self-reliant, and their lives had improved. Some letters showed their determination, some reported their grades, attached with test papers or transcripts, and some expressed concern for my trip.

They really grew up. With my encouragement, Youyong and his younger brother went to work in Guangdong.

In 2008 on New Year's Day, not long before I finished my trip, Limei posted me a New Year card with three photos of her. On the card, it read: "I have grown up!"

Later, I walked to Hubei again, visiting the Ke family for the second time. I called Youyong to let him know in advance. As I was approaching the door, I saw him setting off firecrackers to mark the occasion.

I witnessed a tremendous change in the Ke family. The adobe building of nine years ago had become a three-story brick-and-tile house. The furnishings had also been replaced by the siblings. Besides Youmeng, who couldn't make it back due to his work commitments in Guangdong, the other family members were all at home, including Hongmei, who worked in Wuhan, Limei, who was a ninth grader, and their grandma. We had a memorable family reunion dinner.

I noticed that children from poor families mature early. They learn to improve their lives and change their destiny through their own efforts. Seeing where the Ke family is now, I feel very happy for them.

The Ke family today

Probing the secrets of Shennongjia

On 20 June, I arrived in Fang County, Hubei Province, adjacent to Shennongjia Nature Reserve.

The district is located in the northwest of Hubei. It is the only administrative district classified as a 'forestry district'. The district possesses a unique scenery along with a wide range of animal and plant species. It is worthy of the various titles it has been given: 'species gene bank', 'natural zoo' and 'green treasure house'. Albino animals, and especially the legend of the mysterious wild men, have brought about global interest in the forest. Searching for the wild men was one of the main reasons why I came here.

BACKGROUND INFORMATION: THE LEGEND OF THE SHENNONGJIA WILD MEN

> Shennongjia Nature Reserve's specific geographical location and regional climate have created a lot of natural mysteries, especially the 'wild men'. The Shennongjia wild men are unconfirmed mysterious creatures that have the following characteristics: the same shape, height and strength of humans, full body hair, the ability to walk upright, and high levels of agility and vigilance. The existence of the Shennongjia wild men is mentioned many times in historical records, folklore, witness statements and a vast number of other documents. Since the founding of the new China in 1949, government departments have repeatedly conducted scientific investigations in Shennongjia, only to find some footprints, hair and faeces of the so-called wild men. No wild men have yet been discovered.

The quest for the wild men

In the afternoon, I went to purchase some items for the mountains, including a flashlight, medicine for snake bites, cold remedies and ointment. I also bought a few firecrackers in case I got attacked by wild beasts.

I rose very early the next morning, packed my bag and rushed to Fangxian County Office. The person in charge gave me the county annals, which greatly helped my later trip. A little past 3pm, I went to Qiaoshangxiang Post Office to get stamps, where the staff reminded me that there were winding roads ahead and that the area was sparsely populated, which would make it difficult to find lodging. I hesitated a little but decided to press on.

The sky gradually darkened and it started to drizzle. As expected, there were very few residents about but I finally found a few homes at a turning. Unfortunately, they all refused to let me stay. About ten kilometres later, I found a grocery store. The owner checked my ID and saw my exhausted face and my body coated in mud. He finally decided to put me up for the night.

It continued to rain for three days. Despite that, I climbed over a mountain called Dongergou. North of the mountain is Fang County, and south is Shennongjia Forest.

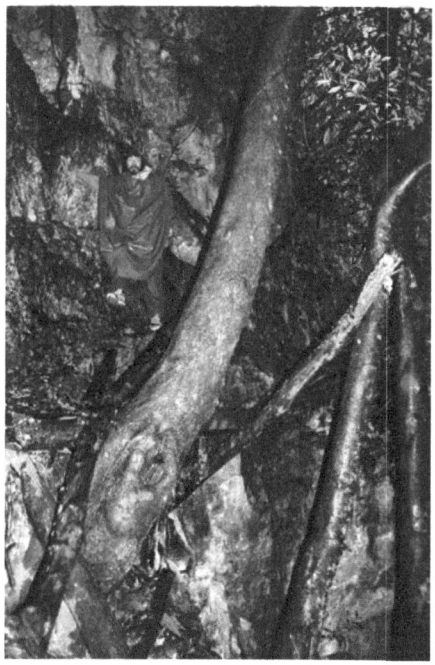

A photo taken with my camera hanging on a branch

After resting for a while, I set out into the forest in the heavy rain. I slowed my pace on arriving at a cliff. The trail on the cliffside was only twenty centimetres wide; below was an abyss of a hundred metres. The rain made the rocks and ground very slippery. I only managed to move my body forward by carefully planting my feet in between the rocks. Even though the distance was just a few metres, it was a real challenge. When I finally managed to cross the trail, my whole body was soaked. I could not tell though if it was my sweat or the rain. People had previously tried to walk on paths like this and fallen into the bottomless chasm below. I was afraid that, if it happened to me, not even my bones would be found.

Although it was a dangerous trail to walk on, there were some delightful moments. I captured a few photos of the waterfalls that looked magnificent in the mountains. About an hour later, I came to a bridge made of wooden frames and steel wire. The small bridge rocked with every step I took, and the 40kg backpack I was carrying only exacerbated the swinging. Fortunately, after a dozen steps, I managed to work out the pattern. From there, I was able to walk faster and steadier.

Encountering a pack of wild boars

As I entered this ancient forest, walking became harder. There were no paths, and the slopes were very steep, sometimes sixty to seventy degrees. Other times, I would find myself under a vertical cliff, impossible to climb. Then I would have to take a detour to another mountain in order to keep going forward, consuming a tremendous amount of energy.

At dusk, I finally found an area of flat ground to camp. The forest was so quiet at night that it was almost deafening. Sleeping in the tent, I could hear a rustling sound from animals passing by. To boost my courage, I held my long knife the whole night, and I surrounded myself with firecrackers wrapped in plastic bags, matches and lighters.

The next morning, when I was packing up my tent, I was horrified to see a snake coiled under the tent. It had been using my body heat to warm itself the entire night. Later, when I recalled this incident, I would get chills down my spine and my brain would go numb from what could have happened.

I had not gone far before I ran into a pack of wild boars that were trundling towards me. I quickly put down my backpack and took out the firecrackers. Before I could light them, the boars rushed towards me. In a moment of desperation, I scrambled up a tree. The boars snorted as they approached me, pushing and humping the backpack that I had left on the ground with their snouts. They left the backpack far away, the contents scattered on the ground. I hurriedly fetched out a bunch of firecrackers from my waist pack, lit them and threw them under the tree.

The boars scampered away on hearing the thundering noise. The biggest boar among the group must have weighed about 250 kilograms. The hairs on its back stood up like needles.

Finally, seeing no trace of the boars, I cautiously climbed down the tree. Because it was my first encounter with wild beasts, my heart continued racing for a while. Until that point, I had always imagined that I would scream in such circumstances; however, now I was afraid to make any noise that might draw the beasts back. So, I quickly sorted out my backpack and hurried forward.

Raw snake meat

Two days later, all I had left was a pack of pickles and half a bottle of alcohol, meant for medicinal purposes. Looking around, I had no idea how much farther I needed to walk, and before long, I realised that I had run out of food.

In the beginning, I eased my hunger by drinking water from the river; however, my body soon began to feel very weak. I started looking for anything to eat. Wild fruits weren't ripe, and their sour and tart taste made them difficult to swallow . With no other options, I pulled tender leaves from the trees and dug plant roots. I understood that the colourful plants were likely to more toxic, so I should exercise more caution before eating them. I squeezed some juice out of seemingly edible fruits and roots onto either my wrist or the back of my hand, and rubbed it to see if my skin became red. If nothing happened, I reckoned that the food was not toxic. If unsure, I would to catch a few big ants and squeeze juice into their mouths to check if they died as a result.

The method worked. Although sometimes my mouth became bitter and my stomach felt uncomfortable, I never got seriously ill. Thinking about the story of Shen Nung tasting hundreds of herbs and teaching civilians to farm, I felt that human civilisation had been achieved as a result of constant trial and error. It was amusing to experience such a primitive lifestyle in today's highly civilised society.

Having eaten so many leaves and wild fruits, I could no longer bear the bitterness and tartness so I ate a few pickles and had a sip of alcohol. My stomach was upset for a few days; I suspected there might be inflammation, so I took some anti-inflammatory drugs. In addition, because my body was lacking in nutrition and energy, I had cold sweats whenever I began walking. I became more and more desperate and worried that I would not walk out alive. It struck me how dangerous these negative feelings were, so I tried very hard not to let them spread further. Because only with a strong will could I survive.

As I was struggling to walk on the rugged mountain road, a snake nearly two metres long sprang out from the thick grass. My low spirits were forgotten and I subconsciously picked up a tree branch and chased it. I used the forked end to pin the snake to the ground and hit its head with the back of my knife. The snake was knocked out. I smashed it a few more times until it was no longer moving.

I grabbed the snake head with my left hand and cut a circle around it using the knife in my right hand. With a firm pull, the entire snake skin came off. Hunger had driven me to near insanity, so I cut off a slice of fresh snake meat as fast as I could and devoured it. The nerves in the meat were still pulsing and I could feel them moving in my mouth. However, I could not care less. Although eating raw snake along with a few pickles and some alcohol made me nauseous, my body started to feel a lot more energised.

I had always cared about animals and the environment, and I knew it sounded very brutal to eat raw snake. Nonetheless, I had no other choice if I wanted to survive.

Later, people asked me why I didn't roast the snake before eating it. I told them that, first, the forest was too wet for dry wood to be found; second, I was afraid of causing a fire; third, I was too hungry to care.

A week later, I eventually emerged from the forest.

My clothes smelled sour from all the sweat and rain, and my shoes were torn open. At that point, I had already walked for eight months and my hair had grown long. As I was drinking from a mountain spring, I saw my face reflected in the water; it was unkempt and withered. I smiled wryly at my dishevelled state. I may not have found any wild men, but now I resembled one.

The first thing I did after leaving Shennongjia Nature Reserve was to search for food. Along the way, pedestrians all looked at me with astonishment. But I had no time to care about my appearance; instead, I rushed to a grocery store to have a great feast.

At that moment, I truly felt what real happiness was like: a bottle of out-of-date beer, two packs of instant noodles, a jar of pickles, a can of fish and a tub of hot water to wash my feet that the store owner had specially prepared for me.

Happiness couldn't be simpler.

Fighting floods in Dongting Lake

In mid-July, I arrived in Hunan Province. The heavy rain seemed endless, yet I kept going forward.

As I was approaching Yueyang, I heard on the radio that due to days of rain, the Yangtze River and Dongting Lake were in danger of flooding. When I arrived in Junshan Island, all the access roads had been cut off by water. The ground floors of many buildings were soaked. The second day after I arrived, all the ships in the dock were out of operation due to the rainstorm.

In Yueyang, I saw dozens of military vehicles moving in an orderly manner to transport personnel and materials to the river. Hunan was reportedly suffering an unprecedented flood disaster, the water level being higher than during the deadly floods of 1954. Public broadcasts repeatedly ordered people to take "strict precautions and defend to the last" and "ensure the safety of the public and the security of property".

Early in the morning on 21 July, I proceeded to Leishi Town from Xintang, Miluo. I saw many small tractors loaded with villagers. Upon asking, I was told they were all going to fight against the floods in Leishi, because the water there was already way above the danger level.

I arrived at Leishi's government building after about an hour, and the news there confirmed my belief that the flood situation was very serious. Hence, I decided to pause my journey to participate in the flood-fighting and rescuing efforts. I deposited my backpack at an inn next to the Leishi Dam and dashed to the dyke.

I came to the dyke at 9am and explained to the commander that I wanted to join the team to fight the flood. Unexpectedly, more than two hundred PLA soldiers at the site broke into applause.

Fighting the flood

Not far from the front of the embankment was the construction of a sub-embankment. The anti-flood team from Xintang County Guangming Village were loading stones onto ships and so I joined them. Although I had become very thin through malnutrition, I could still carry 40-50kg sandbags. The others looked on in astonishment, as they couldn't believe I had such strength. After a three-hour battle, we finally finished building the sub-embankment.

Because I frequently walked back and forth from several sub-embankments and I always carried the heaviest sandbags, I was spotted by reporters from Yueyang TV station and they hurried over to interview me. The municipal party secretary of Yueyang, who had come along to inspect, held my hand and thanked me for my hard work.

On 22 July, internal dam erosion was confirmed in Changhu Village, Leishi Town, and a battalion of troops from Guangzhou was dispatched to the area. I happened to meet a villager riding a motorcycle along the dyke, so I asked him to take me to Changhu to join the troops carrying sandbags. These soldiers were full of energy, and they all raced to do as much as they could. I was lucky to be able to witness the valour and bravery of the soldiers.

In the evening, I stayed with the soldiers at a school. Waking up in the middle of the night, I felt a burning pain in my shoulders: both my clothes and the skin underneath were torn.

On the following day, I continued to carry sandbags with the soldiers. Some of the younger ones got sick due to overwork and the climate. One man from Guangxi had been ill for a few days and did not respond to the medicine he took. I gave him my medicine and he miraculously recovered the next day and was able to participate in the flood fighting again. In gratitude, he would later share his military rations with me.

On 24 July, Division Commander Xu from the armed police came to the embankment for inspection. Someone told him about an outsider who had performed outstandingly in taking the lead in fighting the flood. As a result, he sought me out and was very surprised to learn that I was a backpacker. Asked where my home town was, I told him I came from Hulan, Harbin.

"What a coincidence," he responded heartily. "I'm from Lianhua Village, Hulan, Harbin."

It was good to hear the familiar accent from home. As we shook hands, Commander Xu said: "You see, my fellow, you look great, but a man with such long hair might be regarded as unkempt. Can't you get it cut?"

"Unfortunately, I swore at the outset that I would not cut my hair until I finished the trip," I replied.

He nodded with a grin, told me to take care of my health and expressed his hope that I could achieve my dream soon.

The next day, the flood waters gradually receded. The troops began to retreat, and I continued my trip. During those few days with the soldiers, we established a fraternal friendship. It was hard for us to part. A few villagers recognised me on the road as they had seen me on the TV news. They treated me like a hero and gave me warm greetings; some even handed me food and water.

On 26 July at 5pm, it started to rain again as I arrived in Huangbai Town, Miluo City. My body was exhausted. That night I stayed at an inn costing seven yuan per night and didn't get up until I had slept for a full day and night.

Surviving a python on Luoxiao Mountain

On 18 August 1999, I approached the towering Luoxiao Mountain, located on the provincial border between Hunan and Jiangxi.

This is a national forest nature reserve, with high mountains, dense forests and deep, serene canyons. The pristine natural landscape contains areas of primeval forest, including Cathaya pine, fir and Chinese hazel. Many of these trees are more than a hundred years old. The fragrance of the flowers and trees that permeated the air was pleasantly refreshing.

In the afternoon, the road became narrower and more difficult to walk on. The sky quickly darkened with distant clouds gathering and thunder rolling. Within the blink of an eye, torrents of rain were unleashed. I hurried to shelter under a tree, wrapped my pack in a plastic cloth and put on a raincoat. Because most trees in the forest were extremely tall, I had to keep on moving in order to reduce the risk of getting struck by lightning.

As I was stumbling on the muddy road, I saw a small temple next to a few lofty trees. I could tell from the size of the temple that it had been built by villagers who lived nearby. A plaque came into view as I neared the temple. It read 'Temple of the Seventh Fairy'. From the county annals, I learned that many Hunan people believe in the Seventh Fairy. According to legend, the Seventh Fairy was the seventh daughter of the Jade Emperor, the supreme deity of Taoism. She was the embodiment of kindness and hard work.

I bustled into the temple. The space was narrow, allowing only two people inside at a time, and the roof was broken, leaking drops of rain. Some items had been left as tributes on the incense burner table: fruit that had become rotten, damp biscuits and a liquor bottle that looked untouched. I felt extremely hungry and cold so I decided to drink a few mouthfuls of spirits and eat some of the biscuits, silently thanking the virtues of the Seventh Fairy.

The rain started to abate half an hour later but didn't stop entirely. I knew I couldn't wait in the temple forever; I would be trapped there once it became dark.

Immediately after I walked out, the cold wind made me tremble.

There was no road in the forest, so I just walked in the direction I felt was right. I encountered jagged rocks of grotesque shapes and chilling rivers that came up to my waist when I forded them.

I arrived in front of a mountain as evening approached. Even though the terrain was steep, passers-by had to cross it in order to move forward.

I hesitated for a moment and noticed the surrounding bamboo. I decided to grab the thin bamboo stalks as I walked in order to balance. Gradually, the bamboo was replaced by thistles and thorns. Without anything to hold on to, I carefully stepped onto raised stones and slowly moved forward.

All of a sudden, I missed a step and lost balance. I instinctively grabbed the thorny plants, got pricked and loosened my grip. With that, I slid down the mountain slope. After about seven or eight metres, I caught sight of a small tree and sprung to grab it to stop myself from sliding down further. It was then when I realised that my hands were soaked in blood, and my body and pack were covered in mud. Exhausted, I lay on my stomach, unable to move an inch.

A hissing sound caught me off guard. I immediately became alert and looked towards where the sound came. I saw a python with its triangular head positioned a metre above the ground, lunging at me while flicking its blood-red tongue. My throat tightened, my heart pounded, I felt my hair was almost erect with horror.

The python was about eight or nine metres long and its body about fifteen centimetres in diameter. It was only ten metres away. I instinctively jumped up and started to run frantically towards the hillside in a zig-zag pattern, completely ignoring my exhaustion and pain. I pulled out an aerosol can as I was running and exerted all my strength in spraying back as much as I could. Then I took out the firecrackers from my pocket, lit them and threw them at the python. I also took out my long knife in case it got any closer.

I kept running and running for who knew how long, until my throat was dry and I was barely able to stay on my feet. My heart was jumping in my throat.

As I reached the mountain top, I collapsed to the ground, paralysed from the fatigue. I thought, if the python ever caught up with me, I wouldn't be able to run any more. After a few minutes of dead silence, I mustered my strength to stand up but my shaking legs simply failed to support my body.

I knew, though, that I was finally safe. I raised my arms in triumph and cheered. I had conquered adversity again! Raindrops, sweat and tears all fell down my cheeks.

I began to calculate whether I could make it out of the forest. As I was rearranging the pack, my heart sank – the bag containing all the food had fallen out when I was running away. As much as I wanted to go back, I couldn't. The thought of seeing the python again was simply too terrifying.

As the sky darkened, I turned on my flashlight and held the knife as I walked through the rain-soaked forest. I arrived in Jinggangshan a little past 10pm and found a small inn in which to rest. I tossed and turned thinking about the python. Whenever I closed my eyes, I could sense it chasing me, flicking its blood-red tongue.

The next day, during a conversation with a local old man, I mentioned my encounter with the python. He looked at me wondrously: "You were lucky! It's common here for calves to get strangled and swallowed by pythons. Even though pythons are not venomous, their strength is tremendous. If you do get in the grip of a python, my advice is to clutch hold of your dagger so that, if it does swallow you, you might survive by cutting open its belly."

Using a dagger to save yourself in that manner seemed rather far-fetched. In reality, once you are in the grip of a python, it is nearly impossible to survive.

2000

HAPPINESS IS SIMPLE

This year, I felt touched by the warmth that ordinary people can bring to a stranger like me.

Eating in the wind and rain and sleeping in the open air summed up my everyday life. I frequently felt insignificant in the face of nature.

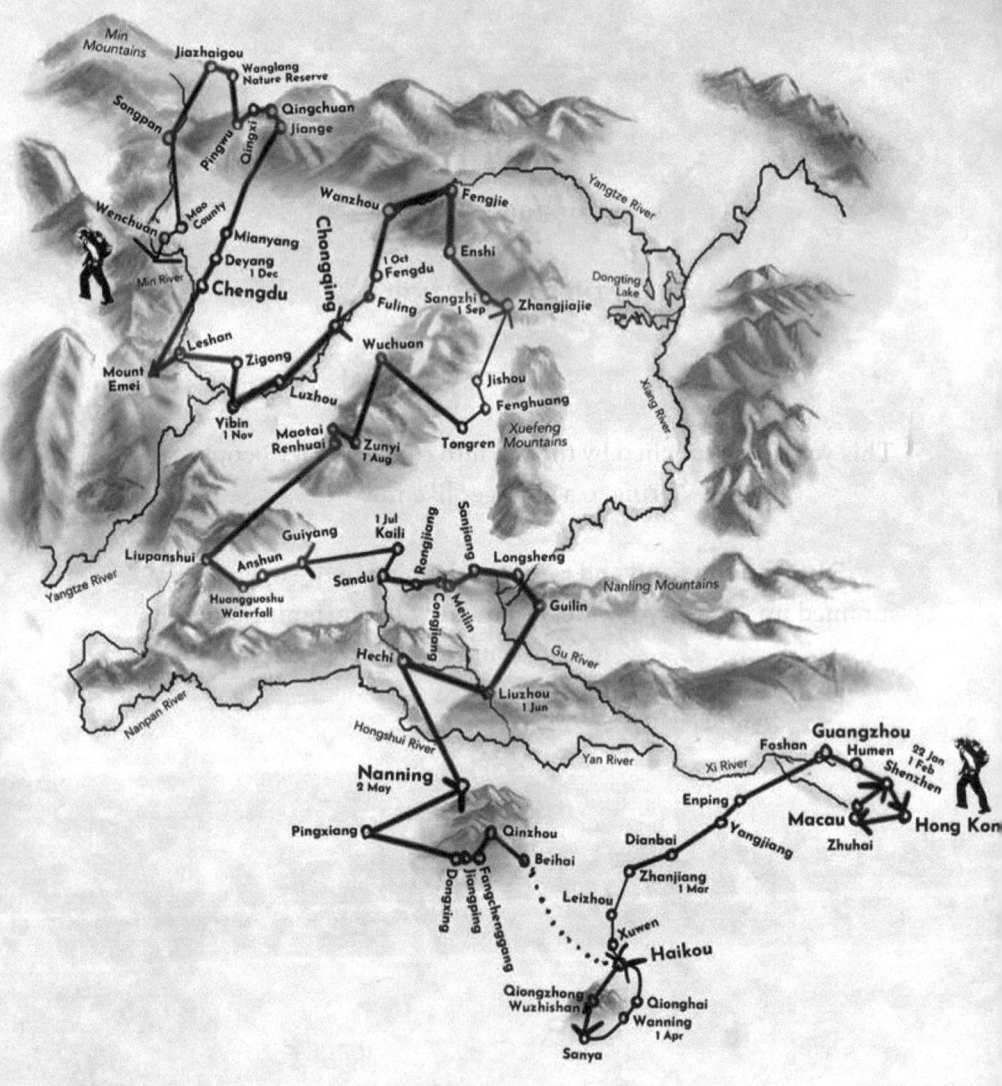

Hong Kong

On 18 November 1999, I arrived in Shenzhen and began to prepare for the trip to Hong Kong.

I had always wanted to travel to Hong Kong and Macau, but I had no clue what documents I needed. A friend told me that an entry permit was difficult to secure and that I had to go back to my registered place of residence in order to handle the paperwork. This meant returning to Hulan.

After several twists and turns over more than fifty days, I finally got the permit on 17 January 2000. I left home soon afterwards, even though my sister wanted me to stay for Chinese New Year.

On 18 January, I bade farewell to my sister and other family members and friends at the train station. I boarded the train from Harbin to Shenzhen. I could hardly wait to see Hong Kong and Macau with my own eyes.

On the morning of 22 January, I entered Hong Kong through Shenzhen's Luohu Port. I first arrived in Shangshui, a new town in the northern part of Hong Kong, next to Shenzhen. Before long, I hurried to my next stop, Fenling.

It was already noon when I arrived. I sat under an old tree to rest. As I was ready to pull out some compressed biscuits, two sanitation workers came up to me and started a conversation. Regrettably, I could barely understand their accent. I told them that I was a backpacker and it was my first time in Hong Kong. They both extended their thumbs in admiration. Ten minutes later, they left after telling me to wait for them.

They soon came back with a bag full of water bottles and packed lunches. Words could not describe my appreciation. That was my first real meal in Hong Kong, a meal full of encouragement.

Then, I travelled through Yuen Ling, Tai Po and Tolo Harbour, before finally arriving in Sha Tin.

It was close to 8pm when I got to Sha Tin. I built my tent under a stone wall next to Sha Tin Haihe River and had some biscuits and dried sausages, a gift from a friend back home.

Finishing my journal under flashlight, I immediately lay down to rest. I was woken by the pitter-patter of rain. It was 1.40am. I didn't know that it would rain when I was erecting the tent, so I had chosen a low-lying spot that meant the tent soon became soaked in water. I packed up and moved to higher ground.

That winter in Hong Kong, the temperature was the lowest it had been for years and precipitation was more than usual. Since I wanted to save money, I stayed in the tent for three consecutive days, becoming soaked in the process.

Horse racing is one of the most popular sports in Hong Kong, and it is a major attraction for tourists. I too bought a ticket. In the evening, I put up my tent in an underground pedestrian passage next to Sha Tin racecourse. I curled up in my tent, trying not to move so as to keep warm. Having been walking in the rain, the blisters on my feet were inflamed. Just to touch them made me groan with pain.

At about 1am, I was woken up by someone prodding my back. Upon unzipping the tent, I saw two elderly men. They explained that they were from Hong Kong's social welfare department. They told me that, due to the cold weather, they were looking to provide blankets for people living on the streets. I hastened to say that I did not need any help. But they insisted that I accept their offer, so I could not refuse.

Later, they bought me lunch and each gave me one hundred Hong Kong dollars to buy food on the road. I was deeply moved again.

Organ donor

During the few days I spent in Hong Kong, not only did I witness the high-rise buildings and rich business atmosphere in this bustling city, but I also felt the warmth of ordinary people. Whether it was the sanitation worker who gave me food, the staff from the social welfare department or the strangers who encouraged me along the way, they were all a great advertisement for the city.

Early the following morning I put away everything, my pack bulging with the addition of the blanket. I was grateful to have it with me throughout my stay in Hong Kong until I went back to Shenzhen, where I ended up giving it to someone who needed it more.

When I arrived in Kowloon, many people walked up to talk to me upon seeing the sign on my backpack. They showed surprise and admiration when they learned that I had walked all the way from distant Harbin. A young man named Guo Daming decided to call *The Sun* newspaper. Soon, a reporter came to conduct an in-depth interview with me. I was told that the article would appear soon.

At Golden Bauhinia Square

After the interview, I walked to Golden Bauhinia Square. There, I positioned my tripod to take a photo.

While I was sitting in front of the Bauhinia sculpture, I spotted a bus parked in the near distance. I was drawn to the words 'Hong Kong

Department of Health Organ Donation Bus'. I suddenly thought of the dangers that I had encountered throughout the past year, some of which nearly took my life. If I were to die on my travels, perhaps my organs could be used to help other people.

Without hesitation, I carried my pack and walked towards the bus and asked for a donation card. On the back of the card were the words 'Regaining new life because of you; donating organs to pass on love'. On the front of the card were spaces to put the name and contact details of the donor.

I filled in my name and my sister's address and phone number. I did this because it would be difficult to reach me during the trip and I would regularly tell my sister of my whereabouts, so contacting her meant contacting me.

I handed the completed card to the staff and told them that if anything happened to me, I would donate all my organs to rescue patients in need so that their lives could be extended. They took the card and looked at me carefully. Their expression was one of curiosity. To remove any misunderstanding, I showed them my identity papers and explained the purpose of my trip.

They said they were surprised because I was the first person from mainland China who had applied to donate their organs in Hong Kong. When I was ready to leave, a middle-aged man pulled me over and said: "Please join us for lunch before you leave."

We chatted while eating. As we talked about my backpacking experience, they asked why I had come to Hong Kong to donate organs. I told them that I hadn't set out with that in mind; it was a spontaneous decision when I saw the donation bus. I had already walked for over a year, encountering many life-threatening incidents. With nearly nine years to go, there was a good chance that I might not be able to make it. Therefore, if anything happened to me, I wanted my organs to help someone, somewhere.

"Please have a safe journey," they said, "and we hope your dream comes true."

A few days later, I finished my trip in Hong Kong and boarded the ferry to Macau.

A tent and a luxurious hotel

The steam-whistle pierced the serenity of the wet and foggy Hong Kong, as waves stirred up by the ferry kept rolling on the glittering sea. On 28 January at 4.45pm, I set foot in Macau.

The places on my list to visit were: the casino at the Hotel Lisboa, the Ruins of St. Paul's, the A-Ma Temple, the Kun Iam Temple and Mong Ha Fort.

A sedan car slowly followed me on my way to the Hotel Lisboa. Before long, it caught up with me and the driver asked: "Are you Mr Lei Diansheng?"

I was startled. This was my first time in Macau; I didn't know I had any acquaintances here. I stopped and so did the driver. He handed me a newspaper clipping and inquired: "Is this you?"

I looked into the car. The driver was of medium stature. He looked kind, well-dressed, and he showed a refined and cultured temperament. With him in the car were two other gentlemen.

I looked at the paper and realised it was a copy of *The Sun* from three days ago. With that, I nodded to the people in the car.

"Where are you heading?" he asked.

"I'm going to the Hotel Lisboa."

"Are you staying there?"

"No, no. I am just going to see the casino."

"We'd be happy to accompany you there. Please get in."

I smiled and told them: "I only walk. I don't use cars."

"That's fine. We'll drive to the hotel first and wait for you there."

After about an hour, I arrived in front of the Hotel Lisboa. I had heard that the exterior of the hotel looked like a bird cage. Seeing is believing; it really was a magnificent 'bird cage'.

The three gentlemen I met on the way were actually waiting in front of the gate, so I walked inside with them.

The hotel was indeed like a palace. A giant crystal chandelier emitted a brilliant light; various works of art and antiques dazzled my eyes.

The gentleman who drove the car said earnestly: "Mr Lei, would you mind joining us for dinner?"

I thought to myself: How expensive would that be!

The gentleman probably knew what I was thinking, and he said encouragingly: "Come on. Let's go!"

Soon he took me to a luxurious restaurant.

The gentleman who drove told me his surname was Wang and he owned a company in Macau. The other two gentlemen were Liu and Qu. Mr Wang ordered a table full of fine dishes. The portions were small and very delicate. We chatted for a long time over dinner because they really enjoyed listening to my stories.

I only realised when Mr Wang was paying the bill that we had spent almost ten thousand Hong Kong dollars for the meal. I was stunned. Converted to Chinese yuan, that would be enough for a year of living on the road.

Later, a well-dressed man came over and handed me a room key.

"Mr Lei," he said, "I am the vice president of Mr Wang's company. Please stay over at the hotel tonight. We have arranged a room for you. It's on the house."

I was a bit overwhelmed and hurried to say no. As someone who had long been accustomed to eating and sleeping in the wild, the food here was too extravagant. Mr Wang and his friends continued to say that it was just out of their hospitality as hosts and that they genuinely wished that I could stay and take a good rest.

As I could reject them no more, I took the key and went to the room. Before long, Mr Wang and his friends came to my room. He handed me two small boxes and took out a watch from one of them.

"This is an outdoor sports watch with a lot of useful functions. You'll find it very useful," he said.

Then he opened the other box, in which sat a golden pen and twenty refill cartridges. Subsequently, Mr Qu gave me a Samsung camera and twenty rolls of film.

We had only met by chance today and I really did not know how to thank them for such precious gifts.

"It was your dedication that impressed us," said Mr Wang. "Money can't buy faith or perseverance. Don't treat us like strangers."

I could not express enough gratitude for such cordiality. Perhaps to them the gifts were nothing, but I was thankful for their thoughtfulness and attentiveness.

When they were about to depart, Mr Wang quietly left five thousand Hong Kong dollars and whispered: "You should try your luck in the casino while you're in Macau."

I knew nothing about gambling, so I walked around and observed. It was such an eye-opener.

The next day, I checked out of the room without saying any goodbyes. Then I called the vice president to convey my gratitude to Mr Wang.

During the day, I visited the A-Ma Temple, the Ruins of St. Paul's, Mong Ha Fort, the Kun Iam Temple and a few other historical attractions. Macau was filled with classic architecture that amalgamated the wisdom of both the east and the west, providing visitors with a visual feast.

That night, I put up my tent in Parque Municipal de Mong-Ha. Once again, the rain poured into my tent and soaked the groundsheet while I was sleeping. Unable to sleep, I sat in the tent until the sun rose again.

Sitting in front of my tent...

As I was sitting in the tent, I reflected upon the stark difference between yesterday and today: a luxurious hotel and my 'little nest', where I truly belonged. Over two days, I experienced the extremes of luxury and simplicity. However, I knew I could not become accustomed to indulgence. Instead, braving the wind, sleeping outdoors and frequently going hungry were more authentic and truthful to my life.

...and outside the luxurious hotel

At dawn, I packed my heavy backpack and walked down the mountain. As soon as I reached the road, I saw Mr Wang and Mr Qu driving towards me. It turned out that they had decided to drive around to look for me since I had left the hotel so quietly. They blamed me for checking out without telling them.

I asked for forgiveness, but explained my thinking: my journey was still long and many more difficulties lay ahead. I could not indulge myself in comfort; experiencing it once was enough. Also, I did not want my friends to spend so much money on me.

They all chuckled once I finished my explanation, probably because they had never met someone so stubborn. Later, they persuaded me to stay for one more night so that I could dry my tent and clothes. It was difficult to refuse their generosity again, so I agreed.

Before I departed the next day, Mr Wang said he wanted to transfer 10,000 Hong Kong dollars to my bank account every year to support my trip until I achieved my dream. He urged me to eat better and take good care of my health.

I gratefully declined his offer for financial support, but promised that I would always remember their kindness. We hugged and parted with mutual best wishes.

My life was constantly enriched with experiences that were sometimes difficult and sometimes incredibly luxurious. Unfortunately, the danger of indulgence was that it might kill my determination; however, I would always treasure the encouraging and warm-hearted words that I would hear along the way.

In search of Xiao Hong's tomb

On the morning of 14 February, the sky was crowded with clouds, and rain fell sporadically. I asked around a few times before managing to find the Galaxy Cemetery located on the eastern outskirts of Guangzhou. The famous writer Xiao Hong is buried here. She was from Hulan, my home town.

When I was a child, my family did not live far away from her former residence. I often thought to myself how wondrous it was that such a well-known writer came from my small and remote village. Everyone in Hulan was so proud of her. *Tales of Hulan River* made this little-known village gain world attention.

Xiao Hong possessed the kind of determination and fortitude characteristic of folk from northern China, which made her seem approachable and revered. Before I left Hulan, I visited the Xiao Hong Memorial Hall to learn about her life. I had brought along two copies of her biography to help me find the cemetery. I gave one copy to a friend during my trip, keeping the other.

Xiao Hong was married to Xiao Jun and then later to the writer Duanmu Hongliang. She endured many hardships in her childhood and died from illness in 1942 in Hong Kong at the age of thirty-one. Some people supposed that her death was caused by a misdiagnosis, while others thought it was the cumulative effect of the sufferings she endured in previous years that brought her down. Whatever the truth, the early death of such a talented writer was very regrettable.

Duanmu Hongliang buried Xiao Hong in Hong Kong's Repulse Bay, so when I was in Hong Kong, I asked around; however, it turned out that her tomb had been relocated to Guangzhou a long time ago.

After Xiao Hong was buried, Repulse Bay became occupied by the Japanese. The cemetery survived thanks to an individual who came forward to protect it. Later, the Repulse Bay area became increasingly prosperous and much of the land was developed and many tombs were damaged in the process. Thanks to the efforts of friends and admirers, Xiao Hong's remains were moved to the Galaxy Cemetery in Guangzhou. As such, it became my goal to travel to Guangzhou and find her tomb.

There is quite a distance between the Galaxy Cemetery and the city centre. I asked many people for directions but few of them knew of its existence. Those who had heard of the place could not give me an exact address. Later, I asked a group of older men who seemed more knowledgeable. Sure enough, a man in his sixties was able to tell me that the Galaxy Cemetery was in Tianhe District. From there, I managed to narrow my search range.

I bought two bouquets of flowers in front of the cemetery gate. But I was soon perplexed on entering the cemetery; it was so big that it was almost impossible to find the exact location of Xiao Hong's tomb even if I were to spend a whole day searching. Finally, after several twists and turns and asking the staff, I found the tomb, which turned out to be located on a hillside.

Xiao Hong's tombstone is about two metres high in the shape of an obelisk, with a black-and-white photo of Xiao Hong set into the surface. I respectfully presented the flowers and paid silent tribute to this outstanding child of Hulan. Standing in front of the tomb, I recalled her last words: "My entire life was subject to disapproval and disesteem. My body is dying and I am not settled… I am not…" Perhaps it was because I had many similar experiences in my nomadic life that her words touched my heart in a profound way.

Xiao Hong's tomb at the Galaxy Cemetery

The people of Hulan had been wanting to bring back Xiao Hong's tomb so that her wandering soul could rest in her home town. I hoped this wish could come true soon. Parting, I respectfully placed the biographical brochure of Xiao Hong on the altar, something that I had treasured for more than a year in my backpack. I bowed deeply.

Passing through Wuzhi Mountain

I departed the outskirts of Guangzhou on the morning of 16 February, moving on to Hainan Province. I arrived in Haikou on 7 March.

On 16 March, I came to the Qiongzhong Li and Miao Autonomous County and found the local annals at the county office. I learned that this area was inhabited mainly by the Li and other ethnic minority groups, creating a rich culture.

Li people in Hainan

The traditional method of weaving employed by the Li women is exquisite. They produce weaves and dyes that are bright in colour and lifelike in appearance. During the Yuan dynasty, a woman named Huan Daopo escaped to Yazhou, Hainan because of the unbearable abuse she received. She learned the textile technology from the Li women and eventually became a textile expert, later being honoured as the mother of ancient Chinese textile technology.

When I was having lunch in Hongmao Town, I chatted with a few Li and Miao locals. They told me that Hongmao contained forty-four villages, over ninety per cent of them made up of Li. They were also very keen to give me directions to Wuzhi Mountain. Fortunately, there was a path that led straight there that would save me thirty kilometres compared with taking the road.

Li in traditional costume

Following their instructions, I began to walk towards Wuzhi Mountain. In Fangdong, a village comprising only ten families or so, I saw some Li women harvesting sugar cane on the hillside and carrying long machetes. The working class are the loveliest people, and I regard them as being just as beautiful and vivid as the Li Jin brocade that the Li women weave.

The Li have unique social customs in which the labourers are all women. At the end of a busy season, these hard-working women can be seen knitting Li Jin in front of their houses. Men, by contrast, tend to sit around on bamboo chairs and chat over tea. This is a unique characteristic of this ethnic group.

The mountain became increasingly steep and rugged as I moved farther away from the village. Later, I simply couldn't find my way. After taking directions from a villager called Wang, I forded a stream, walked across a paddy field and climbed further up the mountain. However, before long, a flash of lightning ripped through the black clouds followed by a rumble of thunder. Within a second, heavy rain began to pour down.

I quickly wrapped my pack in a waterproof cloth to prevent the inside from getting wet. The rain flowed down my hair and cheeks. My entire body was soon soaked. This, however, was not unusual. Walking in the heavy rain on a steep mountain is not easy. The road was extremely slippery with many confusing forks, making it just as difficult, if not more so, than in Shennongjia Forest. While walking, I had the sense that I was going the wrong way. Sometimes I could identify the right direction with the compass, other times I had to judge by experience. After hiking for over an hour, the rain finally stopped and the sun came out.

Having hiked over four mountains, each of them over 1,000 metres above sea level, I became exhausted. The water bottle had long been emptied and my throat was burning. At that moment, I had no choice but to take a sip from the bottle of alcohol I had brought for disinfecting wounds.

Night was approaching. Luckily, I saw a road at the foot of the mountain that was under construction. Some workers there were familiar with the area and pointed me in the right direction. A few kilometres later, I reached the gate of Wuzhi Mountain.

It started to drizzle again and the sky was almost completely dark. I spotted a bamboo hut in the near distance with lights and sounds coming from within. I walked over and saw four Li men having dinner.

They were startled on seeing me enter, perhaps because of my long hair, untrimmed beard and mud-covered body.

I took out my documents and explained that I was a backpacker. They soon became friendly and invited me to have dinner with them.

Becoming less restrained, I saw that there was a hollowed-out gourd in the water tank, so I went and chugged a whole gourd of water. After dinner, I did not bother them further. As I continued to walk towards the mountain, I found a cottage and stayed there overnight. According to a rough calculation, I had walked forty-five kilometres that day.

On Wuzhi Mountain

Early next morning, I bought some instant noodles, crackers and a packet of eight treasure congee. I was ready to climb Wuzhi Mountain.

Wuzhi Mountain is the highest mountain in Hainan. It is a symbol of the province. Upon close inspection, it is made up of five 'fingers', arranged from the southwest to the northeast. The first finger is more than 1,300 metres above sea level; the second is 1,876 metres above sea level. The smaller mountains located between the two fingers are dangerous to walk on.

Looking back towards Wuzhi Mountain

Before entering the mountain, I learned that the leeches on Wuzhi Mountain were abnormally ferocious. In order to prevent them from climbing onto my clothes, I rubbed Tiger Balm and a lotion to treat arthralgia all over my hands, feet and neck. Then, I tied the bottom of my trousers and covered my entire body in clothing as tight as possible, spending nearly half an hour in preparation. A little past 8am, I lifted my pack and began walking towards the mountains.

The first stop I made was naturally the first finger. From afar, the mountain was surrounded by cloud and mist. Next to a mountain stream was a rough path with a lot of exposed roots that were knotty and bumpy to walk on. On both sides of the road was dense, tropical forest, and I often became entangled with twigs and branches. Fortunately, I did not encounter too many leeches; only a few bugs stuck to my clothes occasionally.

During my hike from the foot of the mountain to the peak of the second finger, I did not see any other tourists. It felt as if the entire mountain belonged to me. I climbed six mountain ladders during this climb, five wooden and one metal. Without those ladders, it would have been very difficult to reach the peak. With the peak of the second finger being the highest in elevation among the five, I had an amazing panoramic view of Wuzhi Mountain.

Exotic flowers were spread all over the mountain. The mountain was sometimes misty, sometimes hot and humid, sometimes cool in the breeze, and sometimes whistling with wind. Looking up, the blue sky was so clean and seemingly so close that I could touch it with my fingertips; looking down, the cliff was so tall that it appeared bottomless. It was a wonderful feeling to be able to take in such a magnificent view.

Once at the foot of the mountain, I discovered leech bites on the back of my hand, neck and lower legs. Even though I had prepared meticulously, they still managed to find a way under my clothing.

Leeches often live in grass, on plant stems and leaves. They thrive in humid environments like the one in Wuzhi Mountain. Once they come into contact with animals, they immediately try to attach themselves to the skin and inject their suckers to have a hearty meal. Leeches can secrete a natural antithrombin that inactivates several enzymes involved in coagulation. As a consequence, the wound continues to bleed. Only when the leech is full will it drop off. If you happen to see a leech attaching itself to your body, do not try to pull it off, since that risks leaving its sucker in your wound, which can cause infection. In serious situations, it might be life-threatening.

I have my own way of dealing with leeches. First, I spray some alcohol on the spot where the leeches are attached, then I gently pat the surrounding area. Within a few seconds, the leeches that were formerly fastened to my skin would fall off one by one.

On 4 April, I walked back to Haikou and ended my month-long trip in Hainan.

When planning the route, I decided to split my trip to Hainan into two phases. In 2000, I would take the middle route, walking from Haikou to Wuzhi Mountain and Tianya Haijiao in Sanya, and then taking the eastern route back to Haikou. Seven years later, I would enter Hainan for a second time, taking the western and southern routes.

The only marine ethnic minority group in China

On 14 April, I arrived in Jiangping Town, Dongxing City, Guangxi Zhuang Autonomous Region.

When I was on my way to get stamps from the town hall, I saw a few women from the Jing ethnic minority digging sandworms on a beach. They saw me too and started to laugh shyly. Maybe it was because of my shabby appearance, or perhaps they were curious about seeing a stranger. These women were not wearing their traditional clothing. I heard it was because they only put on their finest attire during traditional holidays.

The Jing is an ethnic minority group with a deep history. Their ancestors drifted from Do Son and other places in Vietnam to Guangxi in the early sixteenth century. At that time, the islands here were uninhabited. Gradually, the

A Jing woman

Jing, the Han, the Zhuang and other nationalities jointly developed and cultivated the three islands in Jiangping: Wanwei, Wutou and Shanxin. Together, they are known as the 'three islands of the Jing'.

The Jing people have their own language and have created their unique script called 'Zinan'. They are well known for their oral traditions, such as spoken poetry and songs. In their culture, there are more than thirty kinds of musical style, ranging from folk songs, to wedding songs, to fisherman's songs. The *duxianqin* is a single-stringed instrument peculiar to the Jing people, with a very beautiful timbre. *Changha* (which means singing in the Jing dialect), bamboo dance and the *duxianqin* together form the 'three pearls' of Jing culture.

The Jing is the only ethnic minority group in China to live along the coast. As the saying goes, 'Mountain dwellers live off the mountain, shore dwellers live off the sea.' Their fishing industry is very well-developed. Whenever a Jing man goes to sea, the elderly, women and children all go to the beach to send him off and to offer sacrifices to the ocean. As the fishing boats set sail, the fishermen on one boat sing to those on another and they in turn sing back. The songs are sometimes emotional and graceful, sometimes passionate and enduring. Over time, the Jing people developed broad minds and became as invigorating as the sea itself.

In the past, the Jing people had a relatively simple lifestyle, and most of them earned a living through fishing. After the start of China's reform and opening-up policy, the Jing started to embark on their own path of diversification, moving into agriculture, fish processing and pearl breeding.

An old Jing couple enjoying the fine weather

On the afternoon of 15 April, I arrived in Wanwei Island, planning to visit the Ha Pavilion, a gathering place for festival singing, ancestor worship and consecrating the gods. Every Jing village has a Ha pavilion.

Sadly, I did not see a local gathering this time; therefore, I was not able to hear their fascinating *changha*.

However, I was lucky enough to have the opportunity to see their unique fishing techniques, involving cast nets, gill nets, seine nets, and some special nets for catching sharks, shrimps, jellyfish and horseshoe crabs. The sheer number of tools and the fine division of work was simply stunning. The most famous among all the nets is the Yu Bo, a sort of bamboo fence that sticks up out of the water. It has been used by the Jing people for more than two hundred years.

On the morning of my second day, I came to a place called Heshan on Wutou Island. I did not expect the white sand dunes to be overgrown with grass and trees. The sand was delicate and silky, white and snowy; against the backdrop of grass and trees, the vast expanses of whiteness looked like snow. What was even more dazzling was the presence of several species of crane, with their numbers exceeding twenty thousand.

When I entered their territory, the startled cranes flew up and circumnavigated the sky, calling and calling. It was such a spectacular scene. I hurried to pick up my camera and took a precious photo of those angels. They hovered and danced in the air, as if they were guarding the beautiful village and its kind-hearted people.

Cranes in Heshan, Wutou Island

Mud avalanche

On 22 June, having passed through Shiwan Mountain and Dayao Mountain in Guangxi, I headed towards Guizhou Province along National Highway 321 by the Rong River, braving heavy rain.

As a result of prolonged downpours, nearly forty per cent of the road had been destroyed by floodwater. Several times, I narrowly escaped being hit by landslides. Hundreds and thousands of rocks tumbled down the mountain like a stampede. The earth trembled and the mountain swayed. Films do not accurately portray how terrifying it is to witness a natural disaster. Only those who have experienced it themselves can fully comprehend the fear I felt at that moment.

What I saw after passing through the villages was unforgettable. Tragically, many of the houses had been swallowed by the flood. Some were missing a roof, others were just ruins. The locals could only watch in tears, seeing their homes and livestock being engulfed by the floods. As they stood by the riverbank, some wiped their tears and desperately tried to salvage wood for future construction.

The mud avalanche

Many homes were engulfed by the floods

The mud avalanche

Looking at the houses washed away by the floods, the leaning trees, the collapsed mountains and the helpless people, my heart sank.

After a long and difficult journey, I finally arrived in Meilin Town, Sanjiang County in Guangxi. I originally planned to get a postmark from the town hall on the other side of the river, but unfortunately the current was too fast for anyone to ferry me over.

Today was the most difficult day by far; forty mudslides were reported. Being soaked in freezing mud all day long, my feet cramped up several times. What was even worse was that my legs often got cut by rocks and they kept on bleeding.

On 24 June, I left Sanjiang and walked northwest towards Rongjiang County. The abnormally severe flood caused multiple landslides along National Highway 321, so the road was closed to all vehicles. When I arrived in Basha Village, the hospitable Miao people used slightly rusty Mandarin to invite me for lunch. I could not accept their kind invitation because their already difficult lives had been exacerbated by the floods.

The inhabitants of the area are mainly Miao and Dong people, most of whom live in the mountainous areas. Most Miao live in the mountains, while the Dong live along the river banks below. Therefore, the flood was a huge disaster for the ethnic minorities who lived there.

The road was covered in debris and tree branches. Even after walking for more than two hours on the highway, I only managed to cover two kilometres. Some parts of the roadbed had been destroyed, so I had to climb over the debris to make progress.

The rain continued to fall but I had to keep moving. When I came to highway section 1008-1009, I saw a catastrophic landslide not far ahead. The entire road was cut off. I staggered in the mud, hardly moving forward. Sometimes I had to cling to the steep cliff with both hands in order to get past the obstruction.

The mountain continued to slide. I remained cautious and alert because a second of negligence might mean being struck by a falling rock, getting buried at the foot of a mountain or slipping into a raging river.

But I had no other choice. I could not back out from the road I had chosen.

'Marriage' in the mountain

In the early morning of 12 December, I walked west through Qingxi Town, Qingchuan County, Sichuan Province. After taking an uphill road, I arrived in Pingwu County. The beautiful rolling mountains made me forget the pain in my feet, if only briefly.

Following the Fu River north, I saw stunning views of crystal clear water in the river valley, green expanses of crops and snow-capped mountains. I looked at the county annals when I got a chance to rest and found many tourist attractions in the area, such as the Baoen Temple, Wanglang National Nature Reserve, Sier Nature Reserve, Xiaohegou Nature Reserve, Beishan Park and Longchiping Forest Park.

On 14 December, I was five kilometres from Jumuzuo Tibetan Town when I saw a middle-aged man with a dark complexion walking down from the mountains and carrying a bundle of firewood.

From afar, he started to look me up and down. As he approached, he greeted me in a dialect with a strong accent. I guessed that he was probably asking where I came from.

Before I could answer, he continued: "You look like a knowledgeable person. Can you help me find a wife?"

I understood him completely this time, so I asked him why he hadn't married yet.

He answered: "What else can it be... I'm poor! Man, if you could introduce someone to me, I'd pay you five thousand yuan."

I was dumbfounded; where could I find him a woman?

He gave me more details: "Last year, my brother bought a woman from out of town and paid three thousand. I am giving you five thousand, it's such a good offer! You know what? If you promise to help me, I'll carry your backpack for a month."

He appeared an honest and straightforward person. It didn't look like he was kidding. However, there was really nothing I could do to help. I explained to him with the help of gestures: "Buying a wife is illegal! If you have five thousand yuan, why don't you start a business or find a job somewhere to get richer? You can marry someone you truly like then."

"I know that. But I live with my mum and her health is getting worse and worse. I can't just leave her." He sighed. "No woman would want to live in this poor place…"

He followed me for a few kilometres and repeatedly asked me to help him. I felt sorry for him, knowing that he was so kind and filial.

On 15 December, when I was passing through a small village in Muzuo Town, I found that all the women were wearing beautiful hand-knitted clothes that were extremely colourful and intricate. They also wore felt caps with long feathers from wild birds that were not commonly seen.

Muzuo Town

In the meantime, I noticed two women sitting on the ground in front of their home. They were busy hand-knitting aprons with wool using a local tool.

Seeing me approach, the older woman stood up and invited me inside for tea in broken Mandarin.

Because I was parched, I didn't give it a second thought and followed her inside. The house was dimly lit and had simple furnishings and a fireplace in the middle. She lit up the fire and prepared to boil some water. Before long, the younger woman came in. The older woman told me that they were mother and daughter, and her son-in-law had been away from home for many years on business.

Later, they served me buttered tea. Since I was so hungry and tired, having the opportunity to drink such a delicious cup of tea was a pleasant surprise. As I was finishing the tea, I looked at them carefully. Even though I would not consider the daughter to be pretty, she possessed the charm of a mature woman. Her mother looked around sixty, yet despite the wrinkles and rough skin, her eyes gave off a sense of astute competence.

The old woman said: "My daughter has a hard life. She has been married several years and she still hasn't yet got pregnant." The daughter kept her head low and continued to add firewood, her rosy cheeks appearing even redder next to the flames.

"Why don't you stay here for the night?" the mother asked as she walked outside. "I'll cook you some noodles."

I felt something was wrong after hearing these words. I turned and looked at the daughter, whose face had already flushed, secretly peeking at me with strange looks.

All of a sudden, I understood what was going on and hurried to put down the cup. I handed five yuan to the old lady and said: "Thank you so much for your delicious tea. I'm afraid I can't stay here tonight. I have to continue on my way."

I awkwardly picked up my backpack and stepped out of the house without daring to stay any longer. Having taken only a few steps, I heard their laughter behind me.

In search of pandas

I arrived in Wanglang National Nature Reserve on 17 December. The ground was covered in frost while the mountains above were cloaked in silver snow. It is said that this area is home to the largest number of pandas in the country, roughly thirty in total.

Mr Zhao, director of the reserve, arranged for me to stay with a worker that night. At an altitude of 2,565 metres, I was awakened several times during the night by the cold despite the presence of an electric heater in the room. When the sky brightened, I got up and started to search for pandas.

Pandas have an exceptional sense of smell, which makes them difficult to approach. Professional researchers and photographers often have to hide in a shelter and wait for days or even months to spot them. Even then, they might fail to see them up close.

I hiked in the forest for two full days and was only able to discover footprints in the snow and faeces that were still warm. Sometimes when I stood on a mountain, I could make out their shapes in the dense forest from afar. Without much luck, I decided to stop looking and move on to Jiuzhaigou Valley Scenic and Historic Interest Area.

The staff at the reserve gave me some biscuits and honey, and a cordial villager named Liang Guohu, who knew the area very well, hiked with me across Motian Mountain.

Next to the mountain lake in Jiuzhaigou

As we walked together, we discussed the nature around and he gave me advice on how to take bearings. After about two hours, we reached the top of the mountain at an elevation of 3,160 metres. On the northern slope of the mountain, all the trees were bare; while on the southern slope, rhododendron trees in bud were growing everywhere, waiting patiently for spring to arrive.

In the afternoon, we arrived next to a cliff. Under the cliff was a clear lake that was set beautifully like a piece of sapphire. The water surface extended tens of thousands of square metres, with mountains enclosing it on three sides. The lake was nearly frozen over. Lakes like this one that sit in the middle of high mountains and lofty hills are called '*haizi*' by the locals.

Background Information: Haizi

Haizi refers to plateau lakes in Jiuzhaigou. It is a term of endearment by local folk. Because they live inland, the people dream of seeing the ocean. Hence, they call the lakes that can be seen everywhere in the area *haizi*, which means 'son of the ocean'.

It took us two hours to finally reach the shore. The lake was surrounded by an abundance of firs and rhododendrons, some of which had fallen to the ground. One-and-a-half kilometres away was the village where Liang Guohu lived. I would be staying at his house that night.

On the 21st, I arrived in Jiuzhaigou, a gully region in Mount Min that got its name because the valley is home to nine Tibetan villages. The crystal-clear lake shone different colours under the sunlight; it was like walking in a fairy tale.

Two days later, as evening approached, I went to forest station 122 at the Nanping Forestry Bureau, where two forest rangers received me. There were no electric lamps so we used candles instead. The two of them prepared a delicious meal for me that consisted of yak ribs and Sichuan pickles.

The next day, they escorted me for quite a distance before returning to the station. After saying goodbye, I crossed two mountains and headed for Songpan County, known as the gateway to Sichuan. It is 3,500 metres above sea level, north of which is Jiuzhaigou, and south of which is the source of the Min River.

As I climbed, I started to feel increasingly sick: my head felt heavy and painful, and I was frequently out of breath. That was the first time I had experienced altitude sickness. I quickly tied shoelaces around my head to ease the pain.

The symptoms continued until evening, at which point I had already entered Songpan County. Being an ancient city, Songpan still retains its ancient east, north and south gates and city walls. The east gate was the best preserved, while the other two gates were dilapidated. The pavements were crumbling as well. Given its poor condition, it was difficult to tell that the city had a rich history of more than 2,300 years.

The next day, I left Songpan and walked south, following the flow of the Min River.

Impressions of Wenchuan

On 28 December, I arrived in Mao County, Sichuan Province. It has the highest density of Qiang nationals in the country.

Their buildings are constructed with rubble and yellow mud. Some of them are very tall, comprising more than ten storeys and ranging from ten to thirty metres in height. They have different shapes such as quadrangles, hexagons and octagons. The windows are generally very small. These buildings slope slightly inwards from bottom to top. It is said that no blueprints are drawn up before or during construction, and that the work is based entirely on artisanal techniques and experience. Known as 'watchtowers', these buildings were mainly used in ancient times to defend against enemies and store army provisions.

The Qiang's residential buildings, on the other hand, are mostly square shaped, have flat roofs, three storeys and are about eight or nine metres high. The roofs are covered in either wooden or stone tiles that extend out from the wall to form eaves, while the tiles themselves are covered with branches or bamboo, yellow mud and chicken manure to provide greater strength. Such roofs keep out the rain and retain warmth in winter and cool during the summer months.

I asked the locals why they designed the roofs so flat, and they told me that they were used for multiple purposes such as drying grain, enabling women to do handicraft work, serving as a rest area for the elderly and as a play area for children.

A Qiang 'watchtower'

The Qiang people still maintain their traditional costumes and customs. Men dress in long gowns with a sheepskin vest on the outside, use either green or white cloths to cover their heads, and puttees on their legs. Women wear clothes, belts and shoes that are embroidered with various patterns, and adorn themselves with earrings, necklaces and hairpins that are made of silver.

On 29 December, I arrived in Wenchuan. Located at the bottom of the Min River Valley, this Ming dynasty city is surrounded by steep mountains on which many sections of city wall are still well preserved. On top of one of the mountains, the entire picture of Wenchuan can be seen, with the surging Min River woven through the city.

The Min has a pristine quality, clear enough to easily see the swimming fish and rock bed below. On top of a mountain close to Wenchuan is the ancestral temple of Yu the Great, a legendary ruler in ancient China famed for introducing flood control; he is said to have been born in the city.

Even though Wenchuan is a place where many Qiang people live, the children here are slowly abandoning the Qiang dialect. Their ethnicity can only be distinguished from the costumes they wear.

Many apple trees were planted on the road from Mao County to Wenchuan. When I arrived in Wenchuan, the farmers were busy pruning apple trees and some women were picking up cow dung on the grass at the sides of the road. Bare handed, they were throwing clumps of manure into baskets. Later they would fashion them into dung cakes and use them as fuel once dried.

On the morning of the 30th, strong gusts of wind suddenly hit the fields, loosening stones from the mountainside. I needed to be careful in order to avoid being injured or even killed by those falling stones. Luckily, and taking the utmost care, I managed to pass through the dangerous area.

A Qiang woman in traditional dress

When I got to Ginkgo Village, I met a high school student called He Kun. He told me that he had seen me on the news and hoped to get my autograph. He also kindly invited me to stay at his home, eager to learn more about my trip.

That night I told him all about my experiences, some of which were dangerous, some thrilling and others eye-opening. He admired my courage and perseverance and was full of curiosity about the outside world.

The next morning, he cooked three dishes for me. When I hit the road again and looked back from a distance, he was still standing by the roadside.

Seven years later, on 12 May 2008, an earthquake struck Wenchuan, razing the city to the ground and changing millions of people's lives. At the time of the earthquake, I was in Anyang, Henan Province. People from all over the country contacted me to check where I was, worried about my safety. For my part, I was thinking about my friends in Sichuan and hurried to call them individually. I made about fifty phone calls, yet only one of them answered. I was not able to get in touch with He Kun either. Was he safe?

I was able to capture with my camera the gorgeous scenery of Wenchuan and the relics from previous earthquakes in 2000; now the memories can only be recollected through these photos.

The ancient city of Wenchuan no longer exists, but I preserved two versions of the county annals in the exhibition hall that I would later establish. I could not help but feel melancholy about the vulnerability and insignificance of humans in the face of nature.

The county annals of Wenchuan

2001

WALKING ENRICHES LIFE

———

All the trouble and fatigue I experienced along the way had been washed away, and my soul was continuously being elevated to a higher level. The blossoming white clouds in the blue sky that were silhouetted against the mountains in the distance seemed so sacred. I stood up and bowed deeply towards Namtso Lake and kissed this wondrous land, hoping that she could give me the strength to keep walking.

Because of this sense of meaning, I found a way to survive time and time again.

All because of a joke

On 1 February 2001, I nearly ended up married because of a heartless joke.

I was walking in the mountains of Yanyuan County in the southwest part of Sichuan. A few women who were cutting firewood greeted me as I passed through a small village. They asked me where I came from, and upon hearing me say Harbin, they thought it was another country.

"How far is Harbin from Beijing?" a woman asked.

"Not far at all," I answered.

"Have you been to Beijing?"

"I used to work there."

"Are you going back in future?"

"Yes."

"Do you have a wife and children?"

"No, I don't."

With an overjoyed expression, she said: "I have a twenty-year-old daughter. Can I marry her to you? You can take her to Beijing."

"Sure! Why not?" I thought she was joking, so I went along with the conversation.

"Is your daughter pretty?" I continued.

"She is! Come to my house to see her."

"Why not!"

I followed her and asked about local traditions. As we were approaching a fork in the road, the women were ready to go and cut more firewood and I began to head downhill. As I was walking away, the woman I had been talking with appeared in front of me and blocked the way.

"Aren't you taking my daughter to Beijing? Come with me now."

I was startled by her expression. I didn't know she had spoken seriously!

I hastened to explain to her that I had to finish my trip before I could consider marriage; and I had no idea when that would be.

She became impatient: "A man should keep his word. You can't just leave now!"

All of a sudden, she pressed her sickle against my neck. The other women flocked over and glared at me with sickles in their hands. This time, I was truly scared for my life. I tried to pacify her feelings: "I have to go to town first. I promise I'll be back in a few days."

As I was talking, I slowly removed the sickle pointed at my neck.

She stopped pressing hard against me and said: "Fine. I'll tell my daughter to wait for you." Then she pointed to the small village at the bottom of the mountain. "My house is the one at the entrance. Don't forget!"

For a while, I felt deep regret. I shouldn't have joked about such an important matter.

Later, when I talked about the incident with local people, they all said that I did the wrong thing because the girl would very possibly wait for me for a long time before she could move on.

I sighed. I learned from this experience that I should not joke with people without knowing their culture.

The last queen of Lugu Lake

On the afternoon of 7 February, I came to the beautiful Lugu Lake.

The lake is located deep in the mountains, between Sichuan and Yunnan provinces. It sits 2,690 metres above sea level, covering an area of roughly fifty-nine square kilometres. The lake has a maximum depth of ninety-three metres, an average depth of forty metres and a visibility of nearly twelve metres. It is one of the most limpid deep-water plateau lakes in China. Several mountain ranges surround the lake, including the Mountain of the Goddess and Houlong Mountain. Houlong Mountain juts into the centre of Lugu Lake, giving the lake a horseshoe shape. There are more than ten islands in Lugu Lake, each a different shape, decorating the crystal clear surface like pieces of jade.

Lugu Lake is described by many people as 'a beautiful painting to its beholders and a wonderland for hiking'. Enchanted by the scenery, I found a moment of leisure that washed away all the fatigue that had accumulated in my body.

Despite the splendid scenery, however, the most mysterious and alluring thing about the lake are the Mosuo people who live along its banks. Wu Chengen, the author of *Journey to the West*, mentioned a place called the Country of Women; in real life, the Mosuo people also established a country that has continued the customs and traditions of a matriarchal society. Knowing that their last princess was still alive, I knew I had to visit her.

The princess

On the morning of the following day, I found the residence of Tsering Erma with the help of local people. I expected her residence to be an elegant royal palace with a large courtyard, but instead it was as ordinary as any other. Appearing in front of my eyes was a slim, petite old woman with short grey hair, dressed in scruffy clothes. She looked quite unlike a stereotypical princess.

Astonished, I began to talk with her. The princess spoke gracefully with clear logic. Her voice, slightly hoarse from years of smoking, slowly revealed a dust-laden history.

The princess was originally a Han girl, and her real name was Xiao Shuming. She was born into a rich family in Chengdu in 1927. After excelling at elementary school, she was admitted to Ya'an Mingde High School for Girls, where she continued to shine. She was recognised as the school's top student because of her skills in singing, dancing and many other subjects.

In 1943, the Lugu Lake area was still in a semi-primitive state. In order to facilitate communication with the outside world, the last chieftain of Mosuo, La Baochen, asked Liu Wenhui, the governor of Xikang Province during China's Republican period, to seek out a sensible woman who had both political integrity and professional competence to become his wife. After a rigorous selection process, Xiao Shuming stood out and subsequently married La Baochen. She was only sixteen years old when she became the princess of the Country of Women.

On her way to Lugu, Shuming's mood was bitter. The distance, being far from home, was nearly overwhelming. When would she have the opportunity to see her family again? However, she did not remain low-spirited for long. She quickly integrated herself into local life, and actively participated in the management of internal affairs and the military expeditions of the Mosuo tribes. In addition, she also brought fifty primary school textbooks and a harmonium from Chengdu and Ya'an to improve local education. Because of her remarkable achievements, she was praised as a 'contemporary Wang Zhaojun', one of the four beauties of ancient China. In 1950, the Lugu Lake area was peacefully liberated and six years later the native chieftain system was abolished. In 1959, Shuming was wrongly accused of exploiting the working class and was sent to prison for ten years. It was not until 1987 that her reputation was restored.

From a lady to a princess, from a princess to a prisoner, from decades of intolerable torment and moments of glory, Shuming had amassed a legendary life experience. She was seventy-four years old when I met her, by which time Lugu had long become her home town. Every tree and bush, every mountain and river carried her deep love for the land. As such, she stayed and would forever protect the sacred land.

When asked about her past, she said serenely: "People's lives are divided into stages, just like the life of a plant. In poverty or in wealth, no one will ever know which part is better. I have lived long enough. My soul shall reside in Lugu Lake."

On my departure, her words still echoed in my head: "No one will ever know which part is better."

Women with tattooed faces

On 17 June, after passing Galabo Buffalo Valley and the Nu River Bridge, I entered Gongshan County.

Gongshan is located in the northwest of Yunnan Province. Its tall mountains and dense forests create a beautiful natural scene. Since it is very isolated, travelling here is difficult. The Nu and Dulong people often have to climb mountains and cross rivers in order to reach their destination. They utilise cattle when they need to transport goods and materials.

It was late in the afternoon when I finally arrived at an inn. The interior walls were decorated with Dulong prints, animal skulls and quivers. Scattered on the ground were a few sleeping bags, backpacks and other items of outdoor equipment. As I sat down on a grass mat, I felt so relaxed that I fell asleep almost immediately. I had a good rest that night.

The next day I got up very early and began to advance to Gaoligong Mountain.

In front of a swift and clear river was a valley road that led to a deep forest. Clouds and fog surrounding the mountain tops constantly changed shape. When I arrived in Gaoligong Mountain Nature Reserve, a staff member told me that it was raining in the mountains. He advised me to stop and rest since it might be snowing at a higher altitude.

Although it was still raining the next day, I was able to make it to a mountain pass at an altitude close to 3,000 metres. With ice and snow covering the ground, it was very difficult to keep walking forward. I finally arrived in Bapo Village, Dulongjiang Town at nightfall.

Because the village is covered in snow more than half of the year, communication is difficult with the outside world. In addition, all the post is carried by humans or horses; therefore, sending or receiving a letter is very costly. It was more than twenty yuan when I visited. Thus the postmark I got was particularly precious.

I visited a few villages deep in the forest along the east bank of the Dulong River. Most of the people here are of Dulong nationality. The smallest village, consisting of just three households, is located between Gaoligong and Dandanglika mountains and is surrounded by dense forest. It usually took four to five days to travel from the village to Gongshan County.

A Dulong woman with facial tattoos

Dulong women have an ancient custom of tattooing, specifically on their faces. Before reaching adulthood, girls were required to have butterfly-like patterns tattooed on their entire face. In olden times, these patterns were deliberately made to look ugly in order to deter men from other nationalities from marrying the girls. Later, only the prettiest girls were allowed to have facial tattoos. Therefore, facial tattoos became a symbol of beauty.

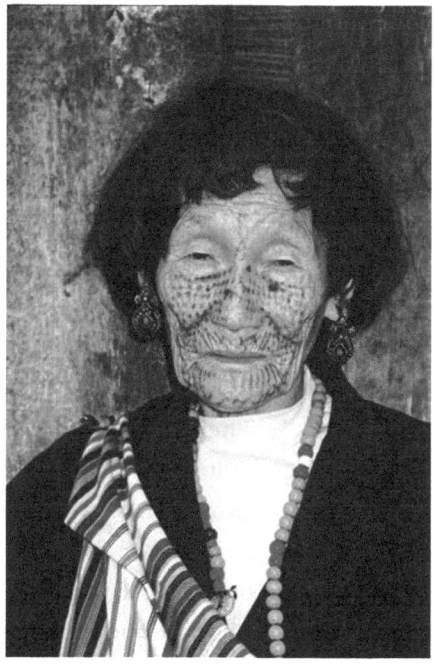

Another Dulong woman with facial tattoos

With the custom dying out, young women nowadays no longer tattoo their faces. There were only forty Dulong women with facial tattoos the year I visited. The oldest was over eighty years old and the youngest nearly sixty.

The villagers told me that women with facial tattoos were rare. Even if I were to find one it would be very difficult to communicate since they didn't speak Mandarin. I told them that I genuinely wanted to arrange a meeting, so eventually they agreed to have a young man lead the way.

We only found a few households after hiking the mountain for hours. Villagers here lived in wooden houses with tiny windows, and the interiors were pitch-dark. Families would light fires in metal drums all year long; however, because there were no chimneys, the rooms were often choking with smoke. Some householders hung the smoke-blackened skulls of bears, barking deer and monkeys under their eaves.

When I knocked on a half-opened door, a man suddenly latched it shut, grabbed a bow and arrow, and took aim at me from a small window. The woman, on the other hand, immediately covered her face with a piece of handmade brocade, holding in her hand a copy of *Quotations from Chairman Mao*.

The young man who accompanied me whispered that they were taking precautions because they could tell I was an outsider. Those arrows were used to shoot animals that eat the crops while the book showed their admiration for Chairman Mao.

The bear bone

After my young companion introduced me to them in their dialect, the man immediately put away the weapon and warmly welcomed me in. They were very excited about the fact that I had come from Beijing, and they gave me a copy of *Quotations*. In return, I gave them some tins of eight treasure porridge, a few links of sausages and some money. The woman with the facial tattoo took off the brocade on her face and allowed me to take a few photos of her. Before I left, they gave me another gift, a bear bone that had been smoked black, which I later displayed in my exhibition hall.

From Yunnan to Tibet

I arrived in Bingzhongluo, the northernmost town in Gongshan County, on the evening of 25 June. Located at the foot of a mountain on the west coast of the Nu River, the town is very close to Tibet. The population is made up of Nu, Tibetans, Lisu and many other nationalities.

It was raining when I arrived. The next morning, Kawakabo Snow Peak, surrounded by towering verdant mountains, was lit up by the sun, resembling a flying golden dragon. The Nu River looked like a beautiful white *khata*, a piece of silk used as a greeting gift by Mongols and Tibetans, that floated in front of the mountain's chest.

A horseshoe bend on the Nu River

The area was abundant with orchids, and I often saw people selling them on the roadside or in rural areas. The flower is rich in variety and cheap in price. Most houses here are built of stone, with walls made of loess, roofs made of wood and tiles made of slate. The multicoloured houses, the snow-capped mountains, the lush greenery and the lazily drifting clouds created an idyllic spectacle.

After visiting Bingzhongluo, I returned along the Nu River to the first horseshoe-shaped bend. On 27 June, I crossed Biluo Mountain, passed Lanping and walked in the direction of Zhongdian, which was renamed Shangri-La in December 2001.

The Olympic flag with 2,008 postmarks

On the evening of 13 July, I was watching TV in a Tibetan's home near Zhongdian County when the exciting news came through that Beijing would host the twenty-ninth Summer Olympic Games.

That night I couldn't sleep.

A brilliant idea came to mind: to celebrate the event, I planned to make a square flag with a length and width of 2,008 millimetres. Printed on the upper left corner would be the Chinese flag, in the middle the emblem of the Beijing Olympic Games and the Olympic Rings. In addition, I planned to get 2,008 postmarks from every province, autonomous region and municipality, Hong Kong, Macau, Taiwan and the Xisha Islands from the date of the successful Olympic bid to the opening of the Olympic Games.

With the idea settled, I called my friends from Dali, Yunnan to have them make the flag according to my design and transport it to me via an intercity bus.

I received the flag on the second day thanks to their hard work. I hurried to the local postal office, hoping to get a stamp from the previous day to symbolise the date. However, the regulation said that the stamp could not be adjusted retrospectively. In the meantime, a few reporters came in and asked to interview me. As a result, the post office staff began to appreciate my way of celebrating the Olympic Games and made an exception for me.

Because of the flag's special meaning, I protected it wherever I went. The flag accompanied me all the way until the 2008 Olympics. Because of it, I was fortunate to be chosen as a torch bearer in Harbin in 2008.

Meili Snow Mountain

I arrived at the foot of Meili Snow Mountain on 24 July. Here stood a stone tablet engraved with the names of seventeen members of a joint

Sino-Japanese mountaineering team who were killed when climbing the mountain in January 1991.

I looked at the stone tablet in silence, mourning the seventeen lives that were devoured by nature. It was in fact the largest number of mountaineers who had been killed at the same time in Chinese history. The tragedy was said to have occurred because they did not listen to the advice of local residents and insisted on climbing. It took seven years for their remains to be found on the other side of the snowy mountain.

Meili Snow Mountain is a holy site of Tibetan Buddhists. It is the first of the eight holy mountains in the Tibetan area and is the most revered in the hearts of Tibetans. Tourists from all over the world come here to visit and to worship the mountain, but few have the fortune to witness its true beauty because for much of the year it is enveloped in clouds and mist. Photographers sometimes have to wait for a month or two, or even longer, in order to get a clear picture. But more often than not, they lose patience and end up leaving.

On my way to the mountain, I met a man called A Fu, a reporter from Yunnan Diqing Television. It was raining, but as we came to the foot of the mountain, it stopped. We both looked up and there was a beautiful rainbow hanging in the sky.

"Lei, look!" he suddenly exclaimed.

The view that I had been so looking forward to was now unexpectedly being revealed as the mist started to lift, revealing the ice-bound skin. Under the setting sun was such a dazzling view of all the colours and magnificence that the mountain had to offer.

A Fu immediately knelt on the ground, worshipping the holy mountain, eyes shining with emotion. "This is the first time I have seen Meili Snow Mountain in such a beautiful state," he told me. "I'm sure it's because the mountain is touched by your spirit that it finally revealed its true beauty!"

Moved by A Fu's words, I bowed deeply to the mountain and vowed to come back to worship it again after I finished my trip.

We waved goodbye to each other after we left the mysterious Meili Snow Mountain. After a day's trek, I came to the border between Yunnan and Tibet.

Stepping past the boundary stele, I entered the territory of Tibet Autonomous Region.

Meili Snow Mountain

Three children in the rain

On 27 July, I travelled to Yanjing Village, Mangkang County in Tibet, where the main economic resource is salt. Salt fields could be seen everywhere.

After crossing a mountain, I saw three Tibetan children walking ahead, their faces purple-red, clothes shabby and hair sticking to their heads. Braving the rain, they were huddled under a small piece of plastic cloth as they trudged on. The plastic cloth, however, was too small to prevent the rain from soaking them.

I caught up with them and asked: "Kids, where are you heading?"

They said they were going to their grandma's home in Lhasa.

The oldest of the three was a thirteen-year-old girl, while the other two were boys, one twelve and the other seven. The elder boy told me that their dad have given them 200 yuan, a bag of milk powder and some roasted barley flour.

When we met, we were still far from Lhasa. It was way too dangerous for them to walk like this with few people around and the presence of wild animals nearby. I had no idea how their father could allow his children go on such a long and dangerous journey. I tried to persuade them go to back.

"We'll be safe because we have the blessings of Buddha and Bodhisattva," said the girl.

"Do you know who Buddha and Bodhisattva are?"

They all shook their heads.

"Daddy said that Buddha and Bodhisattva... umm... they can give us whatever we want. They will help us if we want to see our grandma," the girl said.

Seeing their determination to visit their grandma, I was very worried but could not dissuade them. The seven-year-old boy was clutching his outsized trousers as he walked. Whenever he let go, the trousers fell down.

I couldn't always match their pace as they walked and played, so I gave them my brand-new plastic cloth to shelter them from the rain and to serve as a groundsheet during the night. They were overjoyed. As we were parting, the elder boy said: "Visit us when you arrive in Lhasa. I'll ask my grandma to make you delicious food." Then he gave me an approximate address.

After a small turn, I could no longer see the three children. The distance between our location and Lhasa was close to 1,300 kilometres, and there were several mountains along the way that were as high as 5,000 metres. I really hoped that they could make it.

More than a month later, I finally arrived in Lhasa, a long-awaited city, and I recalled the three children. Had they arrived? Did they go back home or were they still on the road? Buddha and Bodhisattva, please bless them.

Eating twenty-seven steamed buns in one go

I arrived in Bomê County in Tibet on 10 August. After getting the government stamp, I went out to buy food. The road ahead required trekking over mountains and ravines, making the trip very difficult.

The county, located between the east sections of the Nyenchen Tanglha Himalayan mountains, has a unique natural scenery: lush ancient woodland, pure white glaciers and numerous mountain basins.

I set off the next morning carrying ten steamed buns and five baked flatbreads, soon reaching the Zha-Mê Highway. Only open to traffic from August to October, it was the sole road that led to Mêdog County. The building of the road was an extremely difficult process. From 1975 to 1994, the intermittent construction consumed vast human and material resources. And when the project was finally completed, the government held an opening ceremony. However, it took only a single truck to drive over it for the expensively built road to collapse. The truck later became a permanent 'cultural relic' in the history of the Zha-Mê Highway. Since then, the road has fallen into a cycle of 'repair, collapse; collapse, repair'. At that time, I had already been walking for three years; however, it was the first time I heard of such a problematic road.

Tibetans being transported to dig caterpillar fungus

I prepared to cross the Galongla Mountain Pass that same day. The road is sealed off by heavy snow for about seven months a year; road cargo can only be transported during the few months when the snow is melting.

I prodded the snow with my cane and found that it was roughly two metres deep in places. Although I could not make out the right road under all this snow, I decided to take a chance.

Rain started to fall again and walking was extremely difficult; I ended up slipping throughout the day. I finally managed to arrive at the 45-kilometre mark on the Zha-Mê Highway at about 9pm. Across from the highway was the glacier, and I was standing at an altitude of 3,400 metres. It was still raining. Unable to find a spot to pitch my tent, I resorted to spending the night leaning against a large tree, covering myself and the pack with layers of plastic cloth and a raincoat.

Bomê County

I forced myself to stay awake for fear that I would freeze to death during the night. However, at midnight my eyelids were struggling to stay open. As my head tilted, I immediately got up to shake myself awake. That sequence was repeated throughout the night: I occasionally fell asleep and then forced myself to stand up to warm up my body every twenty to thirty minutes. The raincoat did little to help. I was soaked in icy water.

As the rain started to relent, I uncovered the plastic cloth on my pack and wrapped it over my body, finally feeling a little warmth. At that point, I had no more energy to spare. If I encountered any danger, I knew I wouldn't be able to run away.

In the morning, I attempted to continue my journey, only to find my legs and feet completely numb. I had to warm up my body for quite some time before I could properly move again.

I arrived at the 80-kilometre mark on the highway in the afternoon, where the road ahead was once again damaged. Exhausted, I decided to rest at a small shop, dry my clothes and warm myself with some alcohol. The items here were really expensive; things that would normally cost only a few yuan were on sale for at least a dozen times more.

My next step was to cross the Mountain of Leeches. I tightened my trouser legs, cuffs and shoelaces as much as I could, and sprinkled medicated oil all over my body.

Although I had seen leeches before, spotting large numbers of them on the grass, leaves and rocks made me not only fearful, but also nauseous. Squirming leeches were the creepiest sight. They managed to attach themselves to my skin through any opening they could find. Some jumped onto my clothes, but soon they were smoked off by the scent of the medicated oil.

I had to walk on leech-infested roads for several days. It felt like it would never end. Sometimes when I reached a place without any people or leeches around, I would take off all my clothes and scrutinise every part of my body in search of the parasites. A normal-sized leech was half the size of a toothpick, but after gorging on blood, it would swell to become as thick as a cigarette. I found at least a dozen or so blood-sucking leeches on my body every single day.

Along the way, I occasionally saw porters going from Bomê to Mêdog, most of whom were from the Moinba or Lhoba minorities, and some were Tibetan or Han. During a calendar year, they would spend half of the time carrying cargo, and the other half resting because of the snow. Some of their number were women. They often slept in the open during those trips. They would put down a layer of leaves on the ground, cover them with a plastic cloth, and squeeze up with each other to keep warm during the night. Some people, after tramping over mountains carrying rebar and cement for days on end, would collapse to the ground once they put down the loads. Many of them died from exhaustion and rolled down the cliff or into the river.

I walked along the east coast of the Yarlung Tsangpo River for another few days before finally arriving in Mêdog. The county is home to only a few dozen families. All the administrative departments were located in one courtyard. The front gate closed, people could only enter through side doors. I only got to know later that this county was so poor that no one could even afford a bike.

I discovered that the date on the postmark I was given was from the previous year. The staff member looked but was unable to find anything from the current year, so he could only give me an old one. I didn't know whether such a thing had occurred in the history of China's postal service before, but it was surely rare.

After the post office, I found a small Sichuan restaurant. The dishes on the menu were insanely expensive: a small plate of shredded potato was twenty-eight yuan, an out-of-date beer was over twenty yuan, and even a raw egg was priced at five yuan. The prices were so high because all the food was carried on men's backs from other counties. The restaurant owner told me that a construction team had once come here and spent 3,500 yuan on an entire pig that weighed sixty kilograms.

I came here planning to enjoy a big meal, but decided against it because of the prices. So instead I just drunk the free buttered tea and ate steamed buns that were one yuan each.

I thought over my schedule as I was eating. After a while, I looked up and asked the server how many steamed buns I had consumed.

"You've eaten twenty-seven!" she said.

I quickly calculated in my head: twenty-seven steamed buns was twenty-seven yuan. I had spent too much! Each bun was roughly a hundred grams, and yet I still felt hungry.

I paid for the food and went on to buy a few cobs of cooked corn on the roadside to take back to the hostel. This was the most I had eaten on the road.

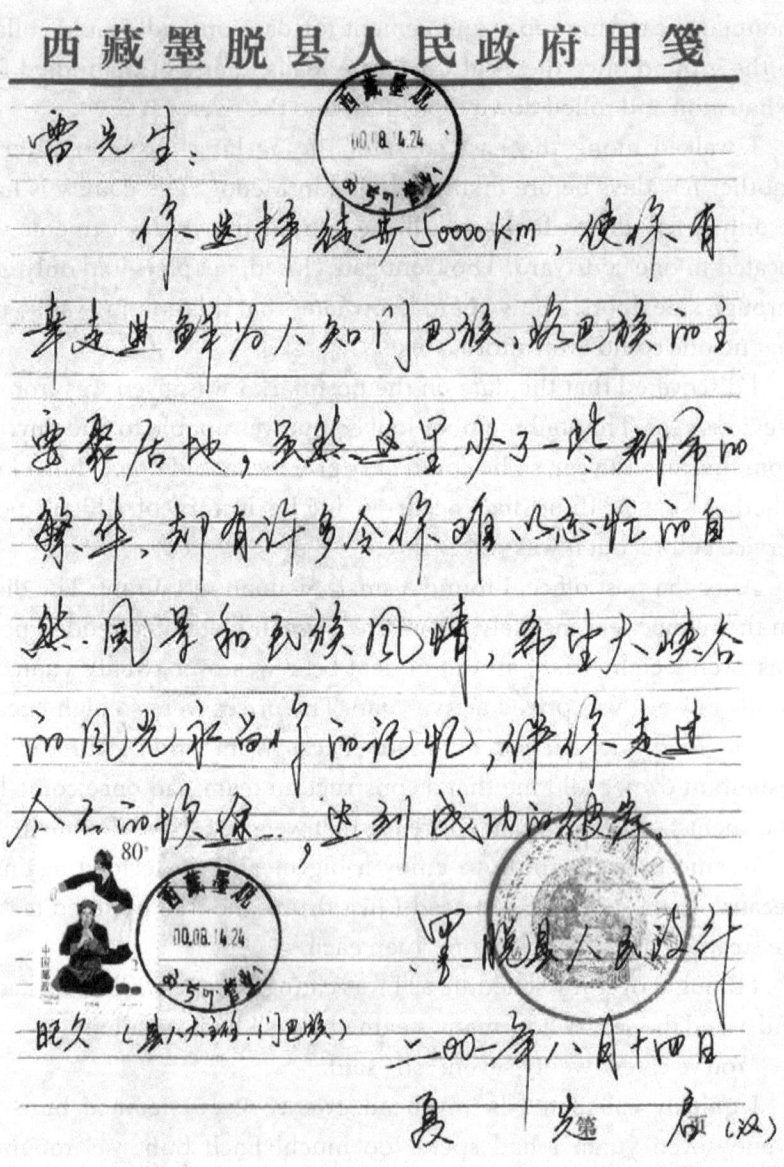

The incorrect postmark

Ziplining across the Yarlung Tsangpo

It took me a day to walk from Mêdog to Beibeng. Located at the southernmost point of Mêdog, Beibeng is mainly inhabited by people of the Moinba minority. The entire village is built along a mountain. Most houses are made out of logs, simple and primitive. I stayed there for one night.

I woke up early the next morning, ready to cross the Yarlung Tsangpo. The bridge had been washed away by the flood, so it could only be crossed by using a zipline. It was very crudely designed: on a tiny iron cage were a few pieces of wood able to bear the weight of three to four people at once. Only a thin cage surrounded the iron frame. When people stood on it, the entire arrangement shook intensely, with the roaring waves of the river right below. If someone fell, there was no possibility of surviving. I was told that children seldom left their homes and many villagers never went beyond the mountain, because they were all afraid of the zipline.

The Moinba people

As I stood at the edge of the river looking at the opposite bank, I was trembling with fear.

Many people were trying to cross the river that day, and so it took a long time before it was my turn. The wind was very strong, making the crossing even harder and longer to complete. I dared not look down at the water below.

Our speed gradually slowed and, as if the zipline wanted to frighten us even more, the cage came to a halt. The only way we could reach the other side was to pull with our bare hands. Even with the combined strength of a few people, we could barely move. Plus, as a result of wear and tear, the cable had become frayed. Using brute force on it was extremely painful.

We nearly panicked. Fortunately, someone on the other side saw us and tugged us to the shore with a rope. Had he not been there, we would have had to painstakingly pull ourselves by hand, inch by inch, to reach the far bank. According to locals, a man and a cow had previously fallen into the billowing river and disappeared forever.

Ziplining over the turbulent Yarlung Tsangpo

I crossed several mountains before reaching Tiger Mouth, a V-shaped canyon with steep sides. Jutting against the cliffs is a winding mountain path that is less than a metre wide. I had no option but to walk on this path, despite it being wet and slippery. I bent down and walked sideways, clinging to the cliff with great caution. I moved forward carefully and slowly.

After negotiating yet another dangerous path, I was finally able to catch my breath.

I arrived in Lage towards evening. I was on my way to climb Duoxiongla Mountain, when a porter on the road told me that the rain was too heavy for it to be safe to climb. So I found a spot in Lage to rest.

Halfway across...

In the company of Tashi, a Tibetan porter, I set off for Duoxiongla. Tashi came from Muli County in Sichuan. It took us two hours to get to the foot of the mountain. The rain and mist blanketed the mountain top, yet just like a hidden beauty, a few waterfalls could be seen that were fused with ice, creating a spectacular effect.

The previous winter, according to locals, more than a dozen porters were killed by an avalanche on their way from Duoxiongla Mountain to Jiefang Bridge. Their bodies were nowhere to be found. I spotted several bent steel tanks scattered among the rocks on my way up the mountain. They were likely the goods that those porters were carrying at the time. After three hours we reached the top of the mountain at an altitude of 4,300 metres. I shivered from the cold wind.

As we were walking downhill, I injured my right foot and it swelled instantly. I could not move for a while from the pain. Thanks to the help of Tashi, I was able to make it down the path safely. We reached the transfer point in Pai Town at 4.45pm.

As I laid down on the bed at a small hostel, I could not sleep from the thought of the perils I had encountered these past few days.

The Yungbulakang Palace

On 2 September, I arrived in Qusum County, situated to the north of Himalaya Mountains, south of the middle reaches of the Yarlung Tsangpo. It would take me another week to get to Lhasa, which was more than 240 kilometres away.

It had been raining non-stop since I entered Tibet. I had to walk about forty kilometres a day, despite the increasingly dire condition of my body. I had only washed my clothes once and the smell that exuded from me

The Yungbulakang Palace

was nauseating. In addition, prolonged exposure to water had worsened the infection in my foot.

I later passed Sangri County, Zedang Town, Ngagzha County and Gongar County, before finally reaching Lhasa on 9 September.

Lhasa has both a traditional and modern atmosphere. The azure sky was decorated with large white clouds, so white that they showed no trace of pollution. On the ground, the snow-capped mountains, meadows and beautiful lamaseries all evoked public reverie. I seemed to have returned to a place that often appeared in my dreams. In the doorways were girls weaving yak wool to make bedding; on the roadside women were breastfeeding their babies and holding casual conversations while basking in the sun. A teenage girl was playing by herself, flashing her white teeth against the sun with a gentle smile.

The Potala Palace

Making prostrations on the way to a holy site

The scenery and people of Lhasa

I later visited Jokhang Temple, Sera Monastery, the Potala Palace and other local attractions. Thinking about my sister's poor health, I bought her some Tibetan medicine in exchange for a ring that I happened to have.

The altitude increased and the air started to get thinner as I walked northwest along the Qinghai-Tibet Highway. My altitude sickness became severe, causing sleepless nights with constant headaches and breathing difficulties.

I arrived in Yangbajing Town, Damxung County at the foot of the Nyenchen Tanglha Mountains on 16 September. This is the only place in China with geothermal power, where the temperature of the springs is sufficient to boil an egg.

The day and night temperature difference in Yangbajing is huge. During the day, there is nowhere to hide from the 'oven', whereas at night, even wearing a sheepskin robe is not enough for people to keep them warm. That night, I stayed at the Yangbajing freight station hostel.

The next morning, I hiked to the mountain, which was basked in a red morning glow.

By noon, the clouds had cleared. At the foot of the mountain was a large expanse of highland meadows. Flocks of sheep were scattered around like snowballs. Not far away, a few Tibetan herdsmen were using dried yak dung to boil buttered tea, filling the air with a pleasant aroma. They invited me to drink tea with them as they saw me approaching. They also reached for a cowhide bag to get me some highland barley.

At about 3pm, large hailstones the size of soybeans started falling from the sky that lasted for half an hour. It was followed by light rain. Finally, at about 5pm, the rain stopped and two rainbows appeared in the sky. The two ends of the rainbows reached all the way to the ground as if they were rooted in the grass. They were so close; I felt I could touch them if I reached out.

The herdsmen who invited me for tea

I spent the night in Ningzhong Town, Damxung County and resumed walking the next day. I was feeling increasingly ill from the high altitude and had to rest every four to five kilometres. I finally reached the mountain top at about 1pm. I was then at an altitude of 5,040 metres. There, I saw Lake Namtso for the first time. Surrounded by snow-capped mountains, the holy lake looked like a heavenly fairyland. It instantly calmed me down with its pure and serene wonder.

I left after taking a few photos of the prayer flags and prayer wheels. The climate here was constantly changing and I was told that there were often wolves, so I had to either find a house to stay in or reach Lake Namtso before dusk.

At dusk, I found a work shed used by a local construction team eight kilometres from Lake Namtso and spent the night there.

Lake Namtso

The sky was especially clear the next morning. The grass on the edge of the lake had already started to yellow, extending and disappearing into the far distance. The crystal-clear water was like a gem inlaid between heaven and earth, absorbing all the beauty of its surroundings. Next to the lake were a pile of Mani stones, which are placed along roads and rivers or piled on top of one another to form mounds or cairns. On top of the pile was a huge yak's head, in the middle of which was engraved 'Om Mani Padme Hum', the six-syllabled Sanskrit mantra. A few pious pilgrims came and went, kneeling and touching their heads to the ground every three steps to show their devotion. The weather being rather cold that day, not many people had come to the shrine.

. . .

It is said that bathing in the holy lake can bring good luck and ward off ill fortune, so I took off my clothes next to the Mani stones and plunged into the water. I silently wished that the lake would wash away my fatigue and guard me from danger. After swimming for a few minutes, my entire body was numb from the cold, so I hurried to the shore and put on my clothes. I lay on the lakeshore, immersing myself in the warmth of the sunshine.

After a satisfying rest, I knelt before the lake and kissed this land of wonder. Taking a last look at the lake, I continued my trip on the North Tibetan highland.

The Mani stones

The best highway maintenance squad

The weather during my walk along the Qinghai-Tibet Highway alternated between scorching sun, rain and hail. Because there were no homes along the highway, I was forced to stay either at highway maintenance stations or in my tent.

On 28 September, a gale swept through the land, strong enough to blow people off the ground. Luckily, my heavy pack helped to stabilise me. Holding on to my cane, I kept trudging forward. I saw a few empty barrels rolling forward unchecked, followed by a group of workers trying to catch them.

It was getting dark and the wind was mixed with snowflakes. Fortunately, there was a small bridge in the near distance, under which was a dry creek. The bridge archway provided just enough shelter against the snowstorm.

The next morning, my body ached all over. Later, I found a frozen brook. I used a stone to crush a small hole in the ice, enabling me to scoop up some water. After a few bites of frozen buns, I finished my breakfast.

Sheltering under the bridge

As I continued, I saw a family residing next to the 19th District highway maintenance station. The host greeted me very warmly. He led me to a chair next to the stove and brought some hot water. I made some instant noodles and was perfectly content. My appreciation for this family was beyond words. When I got up and was ready to leave, the outside was already a world of silver and white.

In subsequent days, the main peak of the Tanggula Mountains gradually came into sight. The snow on the peak resembled a silver tower standing tall and upright, reaching an altitude of 6,099 metres. On 1 October at 7 pm, I arrived at the 14th District highway maintenance station which had the unofficial title of 'The world's No.1 highway maintenance squad'. I decided to call it a day and prepared to climb over the Tanggula Mountains pass and enter Qinghai Province the next morning.

It took me two hours and thirty-five minutes to walk the eleven kilometres from the station to the mountain pass. People at the station had told me that too often they had seen people dying from a lack of oxygen. On a bare mountain like this, only yaks and a few clumps of grass can survive the harsh environment. Their will to live motivated me to keep walking no matter the difficulty. Grass can challenge its limit and conquer nature, I thought. I, too, can persist to the end.

The Tanggula Mountains

Source of the Yangtze River

In the early morning of 4 October, I saw beautiful rays of morning sunlight touch the vast meadow. I had been walking nonstop until noon. Starving, the only food I could find in my pack was a packet of pickles. Fortunately, I also found a small brook fed by the melting mountain snow. I had a simple lunch consisting of pickles and cold water.

Close to 6pm, I spotted a wolf on the side of a hill when I reached a corner of the highway. I took out my knife and slowly passed the hillside. Whenever I turned to look, it would lie on the ground. We continued this pattern for a while before the wolf finally walked away.

On 6 October, I arrived at the Ulan Moron, the source of the Yangtze River. I breathed a long sigh as I took in a view of the clear river and the snowy mountain in the distance. To see the source of China's mother river was an honour, and it made all the hardships worthwhile. I scooped up the water and tasted it; it was rather salty and tart.

Tibetan wild donkeys on the plateau

The next day, I walked upstream, witnessing the small trickle from the Jianggudiru Glacier slowly form into a river, which further downstream would flow into the Yangtze and finally surge into the ocean.

The beautiful Ulan Moron, the billowing source of Yangtze River, has been raising Chinese people for thousands of years.

As I continued north along the Qinghai-Tibet Highway, I saw herds of wild Tibetan antelopes and Tibetan wild donkeys galloping freely on the plateau. It was a scene that was unique to the Tibetan plateau.

My next stop was Hoh Xil.

New 'friends' in Hoh Xil

On 10 October, I arrived in Qinghai Hoh Xil. Herds of Mongolian gazelles and wild donkeys were foraging on the roadside. When they saw me approaching, they swiftly ran away. For the entire afternoon, I walked amid swirling yellow sand. The sand formed into columns, rotated in the air and after a while finally dissipated.

The strong wind made it almost impossible to walk. At dusk, I managed to get to Wudaoliang Town. Although the inn was simple and crude, it was pleasant enough to keep me warm all night.

A giant sand column

It was a cloudless, yet brisk day the next morning, but by 10am it had become windy and dusty again. Grains of sand blasted my face, making me groan in silence. The desertification of the area between Wudaoliang Town and the Chuma'er River had been quite severe. The amount of sand in the air was proving troubling.

At dusk, I arrived at Suonandajie natural protection station. Days of sandstorms and cool weather forced me to stay at the station for a few days. It might have been frustrating to be trapped in one place for so long, but because my body was so fatigued, I took advantage of the opportunity to recover. In addition, I had a great time with the young staff members and volunteers at the station.

During those days, I managed to arrive at Hoh Xil when the weather was relatively calm. At night the temperature plunged, to as low as minus 20 degrees Celsius when I stayed there. On the grasslands and next to the lakes, animals frequently came into the open; the distant Kunlun Mountains constituted a succession of peaks. Yet even in such a desolate place, I was lucky enough to make two 'friends'.

One was a chubby little yellow cat at the protection station. Ever since I arrived, it became especially close to me. As soon as I lay down at night, it would snuggle its way into my sleeping bag, and I decided that I might as well hold it in my arms so we could warm each other. The little thing kept my chest nice and warm every night. I was quite thankful.

During the day when I went to Hoh Xil to take photos, a large golden dog at the station would follow me all the way. Sickly and thin, it walked in a wobbly fashion. By the time we came back, it could hardly move, so I held it until we reached the station.

The chubby cat often bullied the sick dog, scratching its face until it drew blood. Once the cat had finished, it would run away quickly, with the dog chasing it forlornly. I found the cat and talked to it, hoping it would understand that I didn't want them to fight. In the next few days, they actually didn't fight any more.

These two little creatures accompanied me for five days. On 17 October, the sandstorms still showed no sign of abating. I couldn't delay my trip further, so I packed my bag and prepared to go. Before leaving, I patted the two animals and said: "Be nice to each other. I have to go now..."

As I walked, they both followed me for a long time. I turned and yelled at them: "Go back! Stop following me."

Seeing that they had no intention of obeying, I raised a stone to scare them. They reluctantly ran away and stopped to look at me quietly.

As much as I missed them, I did not look back. When I finally turned after quite a distance, they were no longer in sight. Animals are spiritual and emotional creatures; if you treat them well, they will understand.

Later, I often recalled those few days in Hoh Xil, thinking of the sick dog and the chubby cat. They felt like old friends, ones that I cherished and worried about.

My two 'friends'

Surviving by drinking blood and urine

On 30 October, I left Hoh Xil, crossed over the Kunlun Mountains and entered the Qaidam Basin. The environment was brutal.

I didn't see a single person despite walking for days.

I had not eaten at all and had long since depleted my water supplies, so I resorted to eating ants in the Gobi Desert to quench my thirst and hunger. In the wild, if you catch an ant and lick its underside, it instantly releases formic acid, which can stimulate the human parotid gland to produce saliva, a way to relieve thirst. If you are able to catch dozens of them in extreme environments like the Qaidam Basin, putting them in your mouth is an effective last-ditch source of water and food.

However, this was no more than a temporary solution. In order to solve the lack of water, I found two clear lakes on the map. I was overjoyed to discover them. I jogged to one of the lakes and scooped up the water, but was hesitant to drink it. I first smelled the water, which did not have any odour, and then gently licked it using the tip of my tongue. Almost instantly, my tongue started to build up a layer of white bubbles. The water tasted salty, tart and somewhat bitter, a sign that it must contain harmful minerals. If I drank it, my stomach might corrode and burn. In the wild, eating or drinking unknown food or liquids without testing their toxicity can be very dangerous.

The Gobi Desert

In the circumstances, all I could do was to filter my urine and drink it. Because I had drunk so little water, my urine was very concentrated and the smell was pungent. However, I knew that if I didn't drink it, I would die from thirst.

I drank urine a few more times, but after a few days, my body stopped producing any more. At that point, my lips were cracked, with blood oozing out into my mouth. I licked it, and the taste was fishy. Later, my lips began to swell and even licking my lips became impossible.

Days continued without water and I was on the verge of dying. I made up my mind to cut my finger. Blood oozed out and I sucked it, immediately feeling relief in my swollen throat.

I continued to move forward. Whenever I sat on the ground, I felt the insignificance of human life in the face of nature. There was no difference between an ant or a human being. Yet it is in this kind of extreme condition that the human spirit shines, regardless of the fragility of one's body. I kept convincing myself to hold on. Perhaps not far ahead there would be a spring.

On the fifth day, I reached the highway. At that moment, I wanted to holler, yet I could barely open my mouth. I felt like a living mummy, completely drained of water.

I put my backpack on the roadside and sat down on the ground, waiting for vehicles to pass. Whenever I saw one, I would shake my empty bottle as high as I could. Seven or eight cars appeared, but none stopped. So, I decided to stand in the middle of the road, desperately hoping someone could help me. Soon, a car coming from a distance slowed down. However, when I ran towards the car, the driver hit the accelerator and passed me.

I didn't know if I could hold on any longer; but I knew I had to use the last bit of energy to survive. Finally, when another car came into sight, I walked to the middle of the road and frantically waved my hands again. I stood there even if it meant being run over. This time, the car slowly came to a stop, and the driver rolled down the window and excoriated: "What the hell are you doing. Are you crazy?"

I faintly pointed to the slogan on my clothes, showed him the government certification, and said: "I am a backpacker. I have been without food and water for days. Please give me something to drink!"

He hesitated and said: "I only have a little water left and I still have a long way to go. I can't give it to you."

"Please! Even if you just give me some water from the water tank..."

At last he opened the door. When he opened the tap of the huge spare tank, I immediately pounced onto it with my kettle and drank several gulps of water. The turbid liquid had a strong smell of diesel, which I simply ignored.

I indulged myself with water until I belched, coughing violently from the smell of diesel. My body shivered like falling autumn leaves. When I finally stopped coughing, I quickly refilled my kettle, thanked the driver and continued on my way.

Two days later, I was again standing on the highway, desperately needing water and food. This time, I blocked two sedans. A few young men came out from the car in front and yelled at me. However, a middle-aged man from the rear car came over and took a careful look at my letter. Then he said gently: "Get in my car. I'll take you to Xining where you can find a hotel to take a shower. Look at you!"

"Thank you so much for your kindness. But I am a backpacker. I cannot ride in a car until I complete my trip."

"But no one will see you! Why so serious? I won't tell anyone that you rode in my car. Furthermore, this area is way too dangerous."

"It's really OK. Some water and food are all I'm asking for."

He didn't insist any more. The man gave me some snacks, a bottle of highland barley wine and four bottles of water. "We are from Tu Autonomous County of Huzhu in Qinghai Province. I'm sure you will pass our town at some point. Call me beforehand so I can give you a cordial reception," he said with sincerity.

The sun had started to set as I saw them off. I found a spot under a bridge to put up my tent, where I enjoyed the food he gave me. I couldn't feel more satisfied.

After that day, I stopped quite a few more drivers, one of whom was a man surnamed Jian. He often drove on that part of the highway and had seen me a few times previously. He told me that he had no more water or food with him, but promised to give me some the next time he returned. It didn't matter whether he really meant it or not; what he said was already kind enough.

A few days later when I was still walking on the Qinghai-Tibet Highway, a fully loaded truck stopped next to me. It was Jian. He really had brought me food: a large soft drink bottle and two apples! In the vast expanse of the Gobi Desert with no human habitation, I could only dream of such things.

I had managed to survive time and time again. I carried with me a firm belief in humanity and gratitude for life as I continued walking.

2002

A LONG PILGRIMAGE

———

Out in the distance, the mountains that once appeared so lofty were now so small, and the whole world seemed to be at my feet.

When I was in trouble and despairing, countless people reached out their hands to me. It was because of them that I felt the genuine warmth and beauty of the world and had the courage to continue walking.

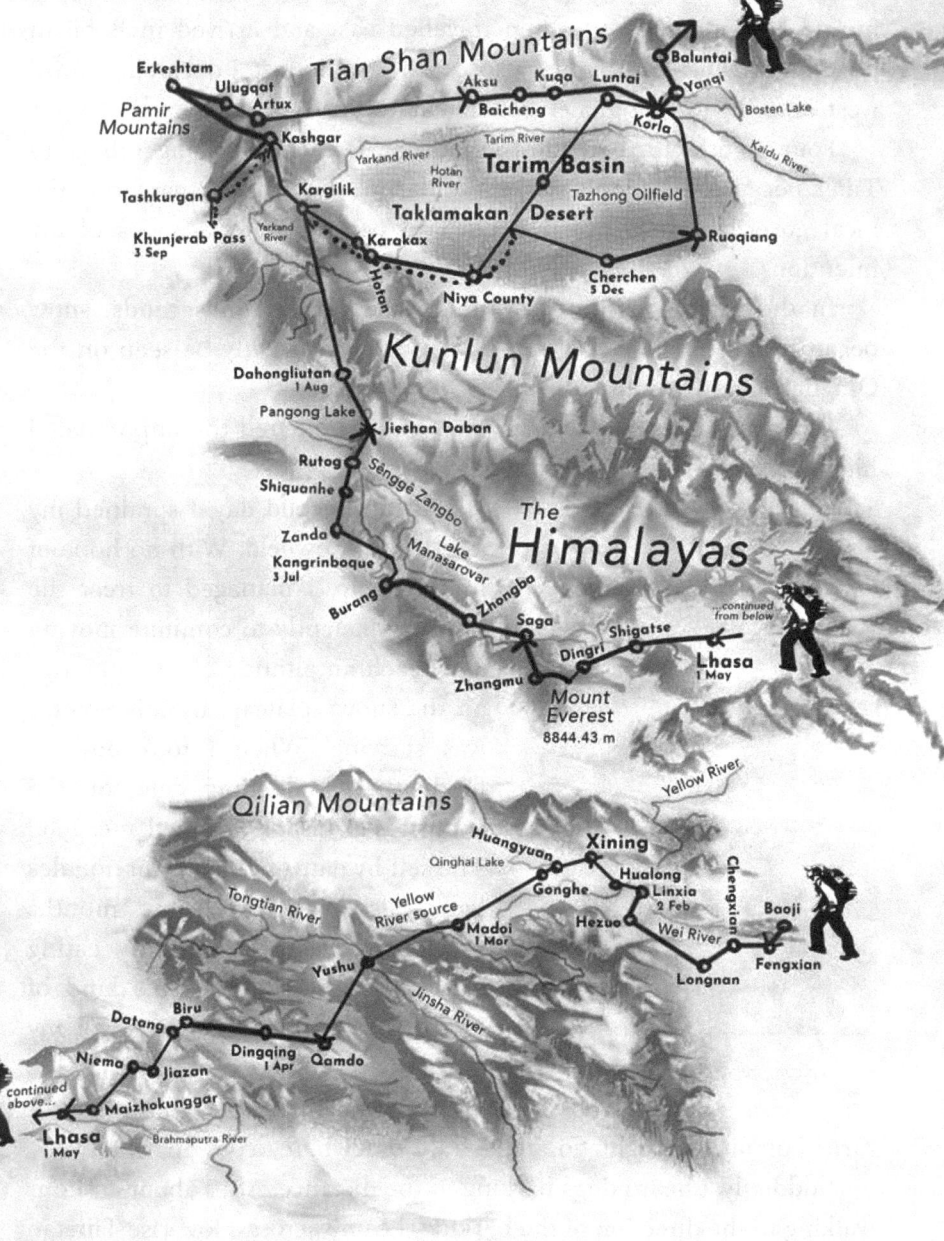

Under the blade of an old Tibetan

After leaving the Qaidam Basin, I arrived in Xining in Qinghai Province in late November 2001. I then travelled east and arrived in Baoji in Shaanxi Province on 1 January 2002. After some rest, I decided to head west, entering the Qinghai-Tibet Plateau again.

Four months further into the journey, I reached Datang Village in Tibet. Because few people spoke Mandarin, I applied for a pass from the local government in case I needed to persuade any sceptics of my intentions.

In the afternoon, thunder broke out and, within seconds, snow began to fall. Perhaps such unusual weather can only be seen on the Qinghai-Tibet Plateau.

Having climbed over a snow mountain, I entered the unpopulated highland meadows in Jiali County.

Eating a compressed biscuit

On the second day, I sprained my ankle in a snowfield. With no hope of finding help, I managed to treat the injury sufficiently to continue moving and reach an altitude of 5,000 metres on the snowy plateau. By this point, I was starving. When I took out my food, the production date of the compressed biscuit stunned me: 1991! The sell-by date on the instant noodles had also expired six months previously. Despite constantly eating expired produce, it was this kind of food that had provided energy for my journey.

As the sky began to darken, I turned on my flashlight, hoping to find somewhere to put up my tent.

Suddenly, I heard dogs barking in the distance. After about an hour walking in the direction of the barking, I came across a low-rise Tibetan dwelling. Two Tibetan mastiffs were desperately wanting to pounce on me. I used my tripod to drive them away and shone the flashlight into their eyes so they couldn't get close.

"Hey folks!" I yelled. "Hey!"

Soon, an old Tibetan man stooped out of the door, which was only about a metre in height. He gave me a blank look as he lit up my face with a flashlight of his own without saying a word. I then shone my flashlight on the ground and said politely: "Can I stay here for one night?"

The old man walked up to me, and, with a whooshing sound, pulled out a knife from his clothing and lunged towards my stomach. I quickly dodged and blocked his attack with the tripod. He immediately followed with another stab, and this time I used my cane to block it. The tense atmosphere made the two Tibetan mastiffs bark furiously at me.

There must have been a misunderstanding. I tried to explain but he showed no sign of comprehending what I said. I suddenly remembered the government pass. In the middle of the chaos I handed it over to him along with twenty yuan.

He pointed the flashlight on my face again and looked at me more carefully, then tucked the knife back into his clothing. I gestured towards the door, asking if he could let me in the house. He also gestured, showing that I could go in.

As I followed the old man into the room, the mastiffs continued jumping up and down. Still frightened, I hurried into the house, inside which sat a middle-aged woman and a teenage boy.

Because of the language barrier, we communicated with gestures and expressions. I showed them the photos I had taken during the trip and the booklet with all the government postmarks I had collected. When the old man saw a picture of a life-size statue of Sakya at Jokhang Temple in Lhasa, he held it with both hands and reverently bowed to the ground.

Later, he brought out a sheepskin bag and from it scooped a bowl of tsampa, a traditional staple food in Tibet made from roasted barley. He handed it to me along with a bowl of buttered tea. The bowl of tsampa had clumps of sheep wool in it, and when the hosts were not paying attention, I quickly picked them out.

The man saw that I was enjoying the food, so he gave me more, in the form of a piece of raw yak meat. He took a piece of it himself and sat down to eat. When I encountered the tendon and couldn't chew it, I would sneak a peek at the old man to see how he was managing. Funnily enough, he couldn't chew it either. He stretched out his neck and swallowed the entire chunk of meat. A small bulge appeared in his neck as it slowly passed down. I decided to copy him: stretching my neck and forcing down the meat when I had a hard time chewing.

The old Tibetan man and me

The old man arranged for me to sleep on a yak skin and I covered myself with my sleeping bag and clothes.

The next morning, after saying goodbye to the family, I thought about what had happened the previous night. If I hadn't practised martial arts since I was young, or if I hadn't prepared a government pass, I might have been killed with the blade. Failing that, the two Tibetan mastiffs could also easily taken my life.

The cold and warm of the plateau

On 16 April, I arrived in Xarma, the birthplace of Gyaincain Norbu, where he was selected as the eleventh Panchen Lama by the golden urn process.

Three days later, I arrived at the foot of a mountain standing more than 5,000 metres above sea level. Without professional mountaineering gear, I would slide two steps back for every step I took forward. After two days of unsuccessful attempts, I returned the same way I came and took a different route.

The Tibetan boy

During those days, I caught a cold that got increasingly worse. The severe headache, nose bleeds and bloody phlegm began to make me fear that I might get high-altitude cerebral edema, in which the brain swells with fluid. I took some medicine, but the symptoms persisted.

As I was passing by pastureland on a plateau, I saw a boy of around five or six wearing split trousers and milking a goat. When he saw me approaching, he passed me some warm milk and looked at me curiously with his large, watery eyes. The little boy had rosy cheeks, common among Tibetans exposed to harsh weather conditions; more precisely, they were almost purple.

He generously squeezed another bowl of milk and handed it to me as soon as I had finished the first. The hunger and fatigue of the journey were soon relieved. Feeling extremely thankful, I kissed the boy's face and hurried on. When I looked back, he was still standing next to the goats, barely taller than them, squinting at me, his dusty face full of dismay and perplexity.

On 23 April, I climbed over a mountain peak standing 5,200 metres above sea level. Prayer flags were waving in the mist on the hillside. Two hours later, I arrived in Dechong Village in Mozhugongka County.

In the heavy snow, I could gradually make out steamy hot springs. I took off my clothes and plunged in. I revelled in the warm spring water, letting the snow fall on me wherever it cared.

The next morning, shortly after I left the hot springs, I saw a school. The school building was a mud-brick construction supported by only a few pieces of timber. With air blowing in through gaps in the walls, it seemed that the classrooms might collapse at any time in the blizzard. Upon visiting the school, I could tell that the children were hungry for knowledge. Unfortunately, I could give them little apart from a few pens and sheets of paper. Despite the meagreness of these gifts, the children cheered and scrambled to surround me.

The Tibetan school

Children at the Tibetan school taking exercise

Because resources were very limited, owning a pen and a piece of paper was a luxury for these children. Having been given some for free, they couldn't be happier. The needs of these rural children were so much more modest than those born into wealthier urban families.

Children are the hope of the future. Whether they grow up in the countryside or in the city, they all have the right to receive an education. If more people can extend their help to those poor children, their fate can be transformed.

Climbing to Everest Base Camp

On 30 May, I arrived at the foot of Mount Everest. My first stop was the Rongbuk Monastery, located at the crest of the Zhuoma Mountain at an elevation of more than 5,000 metres. It was built in the sixteenth century and was once the highest temple in the world. Inside the temple were a large number of well-preserved wall paintings and Buddhist texts.

In order to learn more about the history and culture of the temple, I began to talk to a few lamas (Tibetan Buddhist monks). Seeing that I had a Xinhua dictionary, a young lama asked if he could have it.

I had been carrying the dictionary since the beginning of the trip and it proved to be one of my most useful possessions. I hesitated at first, but considering that the lamas in the temple may need it more, I agreed. In addition, I gave them some instant noodles and soybean milk powder. The lamas were touched by my gifts, so they decided to let me stay in the temple for the night. The entire room had been smoked black from butter lamps, since no electricity was available. The bed was very simple, but living in the temple was indeed much better than being outdoors.

The next day, shortly after the sun rose, I left for Everest North Base Camp.

At the camp, there was a row of stone-built houses that served as lodging for the camp staff. In a nearby open space were a few tents, apparently erected by climbers. In a canvas tent on the other side was the temporary post office of Mount Everest. The office was responsible for sending letters and stamping postmarks for mountaineers from all around the world. It was only open for about two months every year.

Everest North Base Camp

I walked into the tent and explained my situation to the staff, hoping that I could get a few postmarks. There would have been a charge, but the staff understood that hiking across China was no easy task, so they agreed to give me a stamp free of charge. This post office is the highest in China and at the same time the humblest. Therefore, the postmarks have an unusual commemorative significance and collection value.

From there, I set off to climb Mount Everest. To my surprise, there was plenty of rubbish on the road leading to the mountain. I collected as much as I could and gathered it into a single spot, intending to take it to the camp after I came back from the mountain.

Five hours later, I reached Rongbuk Glacier. It would get much more difficult from that point on. Considering the fact that I was not a professional mountaineer and nor did I have proper equipment, I decided to call it a day.

Rongbuk Glacier

I stood alone at an elevation of close to 7,000 metres, looking into the distance. What had previously appeared as lofty and magnificent mountains were now so small that the entire world seemed to be at my feet. This was the first time I had climbed to this altitude. I felt very proud of the fact that I had not used any supplemental oxygen, wearing only a pair of jeans and a jacket I bought in Lhasa for ninety yuan, and a pair of shoes for forty yuan.

Mount Everest

On the way down, I brought back all the rubbish I had picked up along the way. Environmental protection was an important part of my journey and I hoped to raise awareness of green issues with my actions.

The highest road in the world

On 19 June, I progressed northwest from Zhongba County. As I was passing through some meadows, I saw what is known as the 'Polar Milky Way', the Maquan River. It is the source of Yarlung Zangbo River. With the beautiful Himalayas as backdrop, it was an absolutely breathtaking view.

I was about to embark on the Xinjiang-Tibet Highway, formally called National Highway 219. It is one of the highest roads used by motor vehicles in the world.

The Himalayas

The danger of walking on this highway lies in its high altitude. The climate and environment are extremely taxing. With a total length of more than 2,000 kilometres, the road stretches from Kargilik, Xinjiang in the west, to Lhatse County, Tibet in the east. Locals have come up with the following words to describe this road:

> Walking the Xinjiang-Tibet Highway is harder than
>   scaling the blue sky;
> The danger of the Kudi is similar to the gates of hell;
> The sharpness of the Mazha rises straight into the
>   heavens;
> The spin of the Heika circles infinitely into the beyond;
> The bend of the Jieshan reaches out to touch the sky.

Looking up ahead, I saw the Himalaya Mountains in the south stretch into the distance, the Kailas Range in the north running parallel to it. In the middle was an open plateau basin.

This entire region was covered in naturally formed dirt and gravel roads, rugged and with countless forks. Walking in such a sparsely populated place inevitably evoked feelings of loneliness and desolation. As my mind wandered, I vaguely heard someone calling my name. Was it an illusion? As I hesitated, a driver waved frenziedly in an approaching car. When the car stopped, I realised that it was Old Xu, a friend I met in Lhasa! He jumped out of the car and grabbed my hands in excitement: "Old Lei, what a coincidence! I'm so glad to see you again."

"Yes, Old Xu, we meet again!" I was ecstatic as well.

I learned that he was doing business in Burang County, which required him to drive frequently on this road. This time, he was on his way to replenish his stocks in Lhasa, so we had the opportunity to see each other again. He asked me all sorts of questions about my travels and my health, and told me to take care.

During my journey, I often felt isolated, so bumping into an old friend was a pleasant surprise. Before parting, Old Xu gave me three drinks bottles and said: "Old Lei, be sure to come to my house when you visit Burang. I'll be waiting for you!"

Seeing his car disappear at the end of the road, I stood still and relished the unexpected reunion. Such a sincere emotion may never be experienced by people in a bustling metropolis. Perhaps only when you are in an unfamiliar environment, or when you are isolated from other humans, can you feel such unquenchable and inexplicable excitement.

Eating a raw groundhog

Starting from Zhongba County, I spent forty days passing through Ngari Prefecture.

I walked about forty to fifty kilometres a day on average. Devoid of any signs of life and constantly reaching my physical limits for days on end, I started to fall into despair. Soon, I was close to running out of food.

In moments of hopelessness, I always thought about my childhood and the time of famine. We had managed to survive even in the most difficult times. The limits of the human body are unpredictable; and at critical moments, willpower tends to take on a more important role than physical strength. I kept on telling myself to hold on. There was still hope.

One day, I stumbled upon a group of little fellows with short tails who fed on grass roots and leaves, commonly known as groundhogs. They all scampered into their holes as soon as they saw me. There were many groundhog holes in this wilderness; once, I saw a wolf burrow into a hole and seize a groundhog to satisfy its hunger.

After days of starvation, I myself had become like a ravenous wolf. I had no choice but to prey on groundhogs.

Groundhog holes are normally connected. Once they had entered, I sealed off the entrance and immediately blocked the other exit with some thatch and ignited it. Within a few moments, the little fellows inside passed out from the smoke. Although I felt bad, I used a small shovel to beat a groundhog to death. Then, I removed the skin, cut the meat into strips and dressed it with salt. Resisting the enormous nausea in my stomach, I swallowed the raw meat.

The meat had a fishy taste to it. If it weren't for the salt, I would probably have thrown up. Indeed, I would have preferred to roast the meat, but at such a high altitude with thin air and low temperature, setting up a fire was extremely challenging, not to mention the fact that I did not have any equipment to accomplish it.

Alas. I wish I didn't have to cruelly end a life that was living tenaciously in the lonely wilderness. However, in the end, like a primitive man, I sat on the vast and open land and ate a living creature. I had to follow the basic rules of survival.

Pilgrims' heaven

On 25 June, I arrived in Lake Manasarovar.

Lake Manasarovar is the highest freshwater lake in the world, located at nearly 4,500 metres. It has a maximum depth of seventy-seven metres with a shoreline of ninety kilometres. Together with Lake Nam and Lake Yamdrok, they are known as 'Tibet's Three Sacred Lakes'. Lake Mansarovar's name originated from a great religious war that took place by the lake in the eleventh century; it means 'invincible green jade lake' in the Tibetan language.

Lake Manasarovar

Many pilgrims consider walking past and bathing in this lake to be the greatest blessings in life. They believe that the sacred water from Lake Manasarovar cleanses the souls of the five poisons: attachment, aversion, ignorance, pride and jealousy. In addition, it can wash off the dirt from people's skin and liberate them from the cycle of sin. Throughout this journey, I saw devout pilgrims from India, Nepal and Tibet make the journey to receive their blessings from Manasarovar.

As I arrived at the lake, beautiful fish were breaking the water's surface, forming wonderful arcs in the air as they leaped. I jumped into the lake, letting this sacred water rejuvenate my fatigued body and wash away my troubled, evil thoughts.

Before long, I continued my journey. Countless strings of prayer flags printed with seals and scriptures were blowing in the wind. In the first ray of sunshine at dawn, those colourful flags begin to carry on people's longing for happiness and hope, quietly blessing every living creature around them. The moment I clasped my hands to pray, my heart felt touched with consolation.

Ngari Prefecture arouses curiosity among people, especially Mount Kailash and Lake Manasarovar, making it a pilgrim's heaven.

Mount Kailash

Kangrinboque (Mount Kailash), standing 6,656 metres above sea level, is the highest point in the Kailash Range. It is considered to be the head of four sacred Tibetan Buddhist mountains. The peak of this domed, pyramid-shaped mountain is covered in snow all year round, and surrounded by cloud and mist. People say that making a single circumambulation around the mountain purifies the mind. Because a cycle of reincarnation consists of twelve years, circling the mountain every year for twelve years would make a person's life complete and perfect. The most special year is the year of the horse, and circling the mountain once during this year is equivalent to circling it for twelve years. Since 2002 was the year of the horse, there were considerably more people than usual coming to seek blessings.

According to custom, a circumambulation should be made in a clockwise direction starting from the south, then heading west, north and ending in the east. When I reached the north side of the mountain, I saw a fifty-year-old or so living Buddha from Yunnan dressed in a yellow robe who was performing sacred rites. I took a detour around him so as not to disturb his rituals.

The living Buddha

The perimeter of the mountain is fifty kilometres. It takes an average person three days to finish the entire ritual of circumambulation. Devout believers touch their heads to the ground every three steps they take, so their journey might take a week. On account of the loose stones all around, people bring their own leather gloves and wooden boards to prevent injury. When kneeling, their entire body would make contact with the ground, arms outstretched as far as possible. Then they would make a mark at the position of their fingertips, rise up, stand at the mark, and then continuously repeat the same movement.

It took me a total of thirteen hours to complete the ritual.

When I was crossing a mountain pass, a pile of Mani stones caught my attention. Even though Mani stones are common throughout Tibet, these ones happened to be the most beautiful and spectacular I had ever seen. They were carved with various patterns, emanating an aura of spirituality. In such an environment, under a pure and clear sky, and no matter whether you are religious or not, you would naturally formulate piety and reverence from the bottom of your heart.

Seven days later, when I was approaching Zanda County, I sprained my ankle again. As I was limping, an off-road vehicle pulled over next to me. Two men got out and offered me some unguent. In the meantime, a man dressed in a yellow robe also came over; to my surprise, it was the living Buddha I had seen at Kangrinboque. He murmured as he touched the top of my head. Then, he took two hundred yuan from inside his robe and placed it in my hands. Without further ado, he turned and left.

Could it be the epiphany of the sacred mountain, I wondered? How could I have the good fortune to be blessed by a living Buddha? I hastened to put the money in the inside pocket of my shirt. Then I sat down in a quiet place to treat my swollen ankle. As I applied unguent and rubbed the area gently with my fingers, I felt a burning sensation. Soon, the pain disappeared. It was the fastest cure I had ever experienced.

A night battling wolves

On 11 July, I departed Zanda County and walked towards the Shiquan River.

The road I walked on belonged to an unpopulated area and stood at an average altitude of at least 4,000 metres. As a rule of thumb, the temperature drops six degrees Celsius every 1,000 metres above sea level. Even though it was already July, I couldn't feel the heat of summer at all, especially at night.

On 12 July, I failed to find a proper road to walk on in this desolate, hilly area. So, I followed some wheel tracks and used telegraph poles for navigation. In the late afternoon, I found some open ground next to a cliff and camped there.

Later, I climbed up the cliff to survey the area and saw two wolves wandering about in the distance. I quickly took out a firecracker from my bag, tied it to a stone the size of an egg, lit it and threw it towards them. As the firecrackers made a crisp noise in the air, the two wolves jumped with alarm and immediately ran away.

Reassured, I returned to the tent and lit a candle. After I finished writing my journal and eating dinner, which consisted of some raw yak meat, compressed biscuits and pickles, I put the long knife under the pillow as usual and fell asleep instantly.

Deep into the night, I heard a continuous rustling sound. I woke with a start and unzipped a small opening in the tent. Just a dozen metres away, there was a row of green, fluorescent lights twinkling and floating toward me. I was on the verge of screaming. It was a pack of wolves! There were at least twenty of them. My heart began to pound violently; the horror I felt was no less than when I encountered the python back at Luoxiao Mountain.

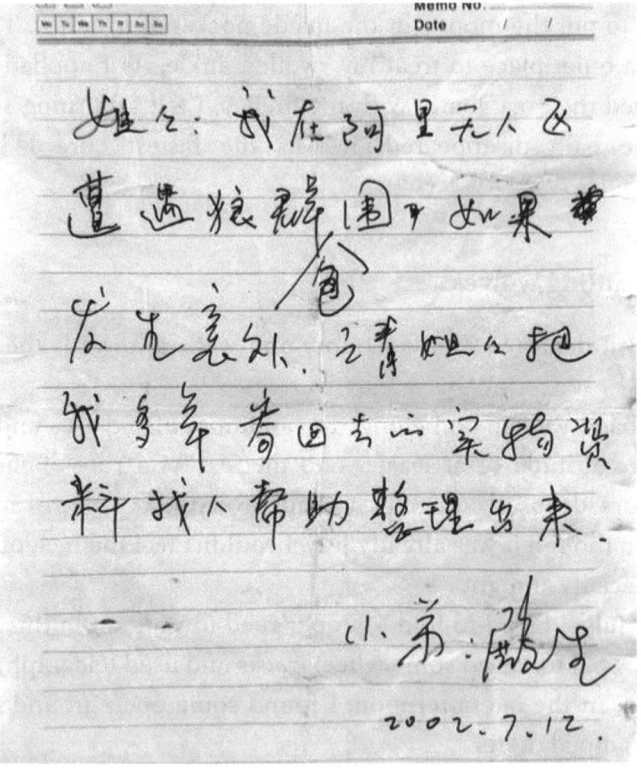

The note to my sister

I retrieved the knife from under the pillow and put it next to me. Then I pulled out the firecrackers from my pack and threw them out through the tiny opening after I lit them. Sadly, most of the firecrackers were old, and they made only a little noise. The wolves were obviously frightened at first, backing away a few steps; however, once the sound of the firecrackers ceased, they quickly surrounded the tent again. I zipped up the tent as the sound of wolf steps became louder and louder.

A few wolves had already come close to my tent, one of which issued a 'whining' howl, and the others circled around, sniffing and digging at the tent. I could even hear the wolves' breath and see their whiskers. For fear of stirring them, I desperately tried to hold my breath. I cautiously opened the zip again and threw out a few more firecrackers. The wolves stepped back again.

By that point, I had already used up all my firecrackers. Between me and the wolves were only two thin layers of nylon that could be torn to pieces with little effort if they laid their claws on the tent.

Without further thought, I picked up a piece of paper and wrote my sister a few sentences: "Today I encountered a pack of wolves and I have no chance of surviving. Please entrust a responsible person to sort out all the materials and documents I have collected throughout the years."

As I put down the pen, my mind went blank and my entire body felt so light that it seemed I could evaporate. I decided to rely on my survival instincts. All of a sudden, as if seeing a beam of light in the darkness, I remembered animals' natural fear of fire. So I rushed to take off all my clothes, lit one item, and tossed it out with my cane.

The clothes fell on a wolf. In shock, it instantly jumped a metre high in the air. As the wolf desperately tried to shake off the burning clothes, the entire wolf pack erupted in turmoil. In no time, I lit two more items of clothes and tossed them towards the wolves.

Soon, the wolves began to withdraw, some sitting on the ground, others running around howling. However, I didn't have any more clothes to burn, so I took out a can of insecticide and sprayed it towards them. Perhaps due to the sickening odour, the wolves backed off even more.

As I was running out of insecticide, I prepared for the worst. If the wolves came back, I was ready to light the can. An explosion might blow off a hand or an entire arm, but I had to do it if I wanted to live.

I continued to spray insecticide outside the tent every few seconds, until the wolves eventually disappeared.

After about half an hour, it was completely silent outside. Even though the tent was full of smoke, I had to stay inside. Wolves are extremely cunning; perhaps they were still staring at me with their shiny green eyes, ready to strike at any moment.

The two thin layers of nylon were all that separated me from the outside world, yet being enclosed in this small space made me feel secure. For a while, I sat there, one hand firmly gripping the insecticide can, the other clenching a lighter, ready to ignite the can at any instant.

I didn't realise how long I held that position until it gradually became bright outside. I carried my knife and quickly went up to the cliff to look around. There were no traces of the wolves. I hurried to pack up everything and left.

The tent and the remaining clothes that were left unburned

Meeting two commanders

The chilly wind on the highland was penetrating. After burning the clothes that had accompanied me on my partial ascent of Mount Everest, I was left shivering in the wilderness in thin rags. Suddenly, it occurred to me that I hadn't just burned the clothes, I also burned the 170 yuan and my address book! The money would have been enough to sustain me for almost a month in Tibet. It would have been easy to take the items out of my pocket, yet I burned them for nothing. On second thoughts, though, I had survived the wolf threat. It was already the biggest blessing I could possibly ask for.

At around noon, I heard a car approaching from behind. I turned around and saw a number of military vehicles. They were being driven slowly due to the rugged terrain. One driver rolled down the window and said: "How come you're still on the road?"

It turned out that they were the same people whom I had asked water from a few days previously. Back then we only exchanged a few words; little did I think that we would meet again.

"Why are you wearing so little?" a young soldier asked me.

"Last night I was surrounded by a pack of wolves and I burned my clothes to drive them away."

As we were speaking, the vehicles stopped and two middle-aged men came out. One of them asked: "Where have you come from? Where are you going?"

I gave them the same spiel I had given to others. One of the soldiers told me that the two men were senior officers, one was Commander Zhu of South Xinjiang military region, and the other was Commander Xu of Ngari Prefecture military region.

I had never met a commander before, not to mention two at once! They looked very down-to-earth, different to how I imagined military officers might interact with civilians. I instantly felt more comfortable.

"Let's have lunch with Lei Diansheng," Commander Zhu said. "You should all take note of this conversation. He has the kind of spirit that you should learn from."

Commander Zhu then asked a soldier to give me a set of camouflage clothes and a flashlight so that I could stay safe and warm.

After the meal, Commander Zhu gave me more gifts, a few bags of rice, pickles and a thousand yuan. Seeing that my body was so weak, he told me over and over that I should eat well to recover once I reached a more populated area.

I was already extremely thankful. He then wrote down a few encouraging words and his signature in my journal: "There are still over eleven hundred kilometres and a few more military stations from here to Xinjiang. If you show them my signature, they will give you the necessary help."

It took me a little over a month to reach Yecheng County, Xinjiang. Commander Zhu's signature helped me a lot along the way.

Commander Zhu and me

My old pal

On 20 October, I arrived in Korla, the capital of Bayingol Mongolian Autonomous Prefecture in Xinjiang.

The extraction of oil and natural gas in the Tarim Basin had brought huge business opportunities to the city, creating a boom in the economy. The city being extremely close to Lop Nur, my desire to cross Lop Nur and the Taklamakan Desert only became stronger.

The next morning, however, I learned that the core region of Lop Nur was heavily militarised; in addition, it was also the site of the first atomic bomb explosion in China, and nuclear radiation was still present.

Sadly, it seemed unlikely that I could enter Lop Nur at this time, so I changed route. I decided to go from Burgur County on the west side of Korla and walk along the highway to cross the entire Taklamakan Desert.

More than 600 kilometres of the road ahead was desert highway, where people are rarely seen, and food and water are hard to find. In order to save energy carrying my heavy pack, I decided to buy a wheelbarrow at a local market in Korla for a hundred yuan. I also bought a pump, spare tyres and some additional parts for emergency use.

From that day on, the wheelbarrow stayed with me day and night like a partner. When the wind blew, I would fix the tent to the barrow and let it protect me from sand and wind; when the burning hot sun left me nowhere to hide, I put my head under it to escape the heat.

The barrow accompanied me across the entire Taklamakan Desert, escorted me through the Tian Shan and Qinling mountains, and followed me in vast forests and grasslands. My 'old pal' spent over two years with me, got through more than seventy tyres, travelled nearly 17,000 kilometres and kept me company until I reached my home town of Harbin.

I forged a deep friendship with my old pal, so much so that when a friend wanted to buy it from me despite its worn-out condition, I could not bear to let it go. I have, of course, kept it in my exhibition hall. Every time I see it, vivid memories of the time we spent together come flooding back.

My old pal

Lost and found

On 15 November, I entered Hotan Prefecture, best known for its raw jade. Two days later, I went to the bazaar, where a variety of souvenirs, handicrafts and Hetian jade (nephrite) could be found.

Hotan is located in southwestern Xinjiang. Uyghurs make up about ninety-six per cent of the population. Since most of them don't speak Mandarin, I asked Zhu Huibin from the inn to help translate at the market. Her mother being Uyghur and her father being Han, she was fluent in both Uyghur and Mandarin.

In the market, the huge variety of jade was astonishing. Having taken several photos, I fumbled for my notebook. I couldn't find it. It contained more than eighty postmarks that I had collected over the past three months in Xinjiang!

Huibin and I immediately started searching the streets we had passed, but there was no trace of it. Someone suggested we use the market's public address system; so, we went there for help. Soon, the loud and urgent voice of an announcer came through.

While we were waiting, we also went to a nearby police station to seek help. Two policemen returned with us and repeatedly spoke with pedestrians in Uygur, trying to help us find the notebook.

The police get involved

As the sky darkened, there were fewer and fewer people in the market. Workers were already clearing away the rubbish, yet the notebook was still nowhere to be found. I used the flashlight to look for the notebook one last time but left in frustration.

The second day, Huibin advised me to go to the TV station to spread my message to more people.

"It definitely won't be cheap if we want help from the TV station," I said.

"I know. But since your notebook is so important, it doesn't hurt to give it a try."

Luckily, when the staff members learned about my story, they agreed to broadcast scrolling text on their channel.

However, the entire day had gone by and I still didn't hear anything from them.

I couldn't delay my schedule any further so I planned to leave the next morning. Before departing, Huibin tried to console me: "Lei, don't worry too much about it. I'll keep searching for your notebook. Once there's any news from the TV station, I'll let you know right away."

With gratitude, I walked towards Karakax County.

It was about noon, and as I kept on thinking about the notebook, I heard someone calling my name. I turned and saw Huibin getting out of a bus that had stopped next to me. She was holding the notebook, her face was flushed with excitement.

"Lei, I found it!" she exclaimed.

I took the notebook with both hands and became so overjoyed that I could not speak. After we had both calmed down, we sat on the side of the road while Huibin told me the story.

It turned out that shortly after I left Hotan, a worker at the TV station called Huibin, telling her that a few young fellows had brought the notebook to the station and asked for 800 yuan in return. Huibin then rushed to the TV station to explain to the young men that the person who had lost the notebook was just an ordinary person who didn't have much money. She said she could give them 200 yuan, but knowing the value of the notebook, they insisted on at least 500 yuan.

Huibin returning the notebook to me

Meanwhile, the worker at the station secretly called the police. Before long, a few officers arrived.

Seeing the situation, the young men wanted to sneak away; however, they got stopped by the police. "Leave the notebook and we will give you a hundred yuan. If you refuse, we'll have to go back to the police station to do a thorough investigation." Terrified, they took the money and left immediately.

Having secured the notebook, Huibin hurried to catch the bus home.

The story filled my mind with a myriad of thoughts. Whenever I was in trouble or despair, countless people reached out their hands to me. It was because of folk like Huibin that I felt the genuine feelings and beauty of the world and had the courage to continue walking.

With the highway as background, Huibin and I took a photo together that will always be memorable to me.

2003
A MESMERISING TALE

―――

In that pure, distant and mesmerising melody, my mind wandered to the Kanas Mountains and lakes.

That night I didn't sleep, for fear of not being able to ever wake up again.

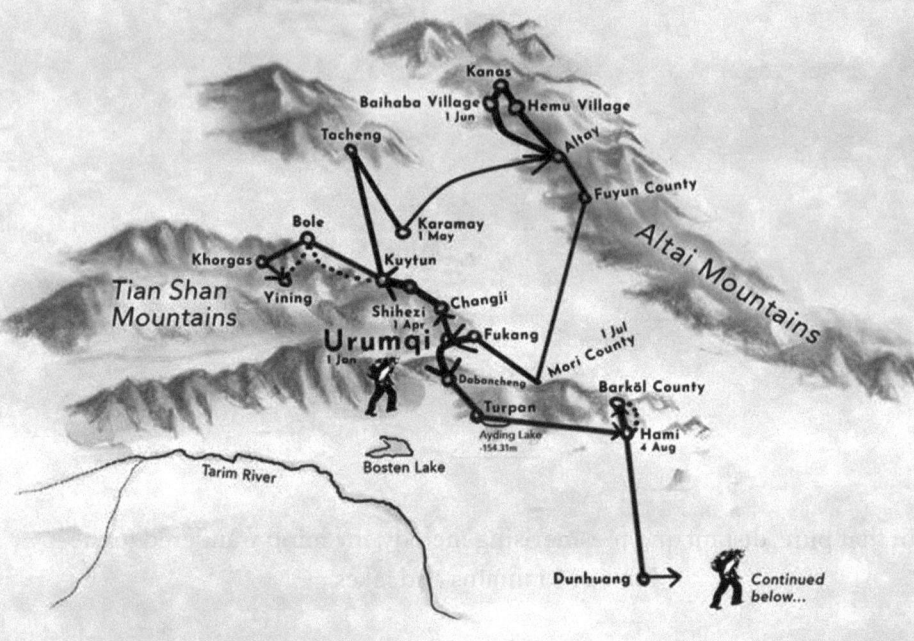
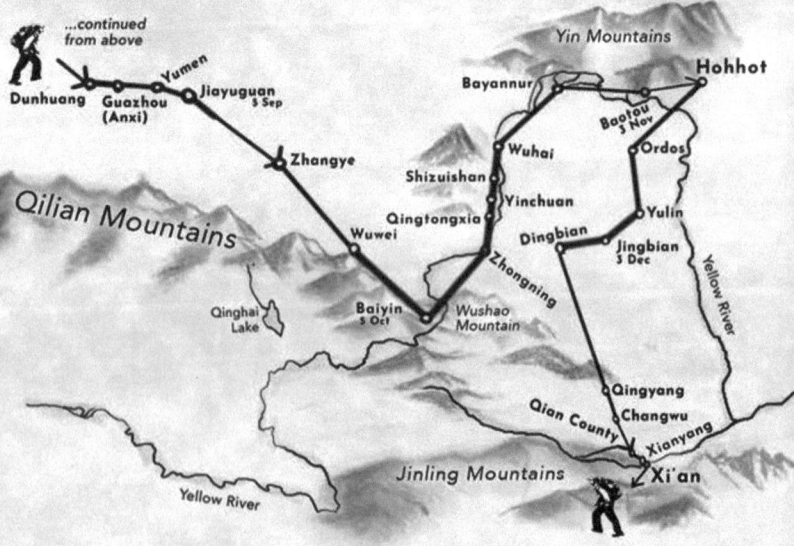

The only Tuvan who can play the chuur

On 28 May 2003, I crossed the Bu'erjin Bridge and continued north in the barren desert.

By noon, the sun had scorched the land and my clothes were soaked in sweat. After crossing steep mountains, I arrived at the border defence station in Baihaba Village, which was widely known as 'the first sentry post in northwestern China'. There, I was fortunate to be accompanied by Zhou Yongxiang, a medical officer, to visit the boundary monument between China and Kazakhstan.

The monument on China's side is located on a small hill on the east bank of the Akehaba River. Not far ahead is the tomb of a Soviet general. And on the west bank, only a few steps away, stands the boundary monument of Kazakhstan.

Ogival wooden houses in Baihaba

The architecture of Baihaba consists mainly of ogival houses whose walls and ceilings are all made of wood. The roofs are generally made from round logs that are as thick as ten centimetres and are formed into a triangular shape. The locals told me that, because of frequent snowstorms, the steep roofs helped reduce the amount of accumulated snow and facilitated in drainage, keeping the houses safe to live in. In the interior, every household looked like a museum of arts and crafts, with tapestries on the beds, embroidery on the walls and an exquisite stove in the centre of the room.

The local residents consist mainly of Tuvans and Kazakhs. Legend has it that the Tuvans are descendants of Mongols dating back to Genghis Khan's expedition to the west. They led a primitive and isolated life for thousands of years. The reason why they settled down here was because of the idyllic beauty of Kanas. It was only in recent years, with the arrival of many tourists, that the area's tranquillity was shattered. Residents started to give up the raising of livestock and switched to opening family hotels. The villagers are both generous and hospitable. Even though tourists find it difficult to understand their language, they always appreciate their enthusiasm and simplicity.

I arrived at Kanas Lake the next day. Due to the SARS outbreak, there were only a few visitors about.

Yeerdexi

In the evening, I arrived in a nearby village to visit a well-known person among Tuvans, Yeerdexi.

Yeerdexi is the only Tuvan person who can play the *chuur*, a traditional end-blown flute made from the stems of a type of grass grown only locally. There are three holes in the bottom of a *chuur*. It was quite fascinating to think about the fact that people could accurately identify intonations through these holes.

In his small courtyard, Yeerdexi played a melody on the *chuur* that was both ancient and mysterious. His face glittered with youth. As I listened, I thought I could hear the sound of a bear running through the jungle or of a hunter chasing his prey. In that pure, distant and mesmerising melody, my mind wandered to the Kanas Mountains and lakes.

While we were chatting, the old man informed me that the Tuvans did not have written characters and therefore the music was passed by word of mouth. He had grown up in the wild, grazing cattle and sheep, where he slowly realised that the ancestral music was in truth the voice of nature. Apart from being able to play the three songs handed down by his ancestors, he created two new songs himself.

Despite his own achievements, he was worried that there would be no one to take on the mantle. It requires great skill to play the *chuur*; normally it would take at least three years just to make a sound. He had been personally instructing his son and another young man to play, yet neither of them seemed to be interested. His grief grew heavier.

On 3 June, I left Kanas. While observing the beauty of nature, my thoughts were still occupied by the melodic *chuur* and the deep and melancholic look in Yeerdexi's eyes.

The Flaming Mountains and Ayding Lake

Heading south, I passed the Tian Shan Mountains and the town of Dabancheng that featured in a famous song written by Wang Luobin; in late July, I arrived at the Flaming Mountains located on the south side of the Tian Shan range.

The Flaming Mountains got their name from the red sandstone. In midsummer, the sandstone shines brightly in the sunlight, shimmering in the heat, like an enormous ball of flame burning in the air. In *Journey to the West*, the story of Sun Wukong (the Monkey King) borrowing a palm-leaf fan adds another layer of mystery to the Flaming Mountains.

The Tian Shan Mountains

The Flaming Mountains

From afar, the burning hot Flaming Mountains and the distant grey Gobi Desert formed a delightful contrast. When I walked to the southwest slope of the mountain, I saw many people attempting to bury their bodies in the dark red sand, with only their heads visible. I soon learned that they were trying sand therapy. Reputedly, the minerals in the sand are an effective treatment for pain when the daytime temperature reaches 60 or 70 degrees Celsius. As a result, many patients with arthritis, rheumatism and skin conditions come all the way here, hoping to alleviate their condition with the magical sand.

This was such a rare opportunity, so I had to experience the magic myself. When I first laid down on the sand, I felt extremely hot. Soon afterwards, though, I could feel the coldness of my body, the eczema, the soreness and the pain being slowly sucked away. I felt this was a gift from Earth, sweeping away the exhaustion of body and mind that had built up within me.

Standing over the karez

On the following day, I saw a major feature of the Turpan region, the karez. It was said to be the second largest water conservation project in ancient China after Dujiangyan. Due to the scorching heat and extreme dryness in the Turpan Depression, most of the water that melts from the Tian Shan Mountains quickly evaporates. Previous generations dug a well every few hundred metres next to the river to overcome this problem. As a result, a network of water channels formed, connecting them to Turpan and Hami. The water underground was naturally filtered and free from pollution. It provided natural heat in winter and natural chill in summer. To this day, nearly half of the local people still drink water from the karez.

I tasted the karez water. It was cool and sweet, so I filled a bottle to take with me.

At dusk, I arrived at the lowest point in China, Ayding Lake. It stands 154 metres below sea level, and is located thirty kilometres southeast of the Turpan Depression. At the time, industrial brine was being mined on a large scale, and it is said that it can cause serious skin burns.

Ayding Lake

Ayding Lake, the lowest point in China

I halted next to the lake, my mind wandering. A year ago, I climbed to an altitude of nearly 7,000 metres, and today here I was at the lowest altitude in China. A challenge like this did not just convey to me a sense of conquering nature, but a breakthrough in terms of both my physical agility and personal beliefs.

The sandstorm

On 4 August, I arrived in Hami. Walking in a southeasterly direction, I reached the Hexi Corridor in mid-August, among the hottest days in summer.

The majesty and miracles of nature are fully displayed in the Hexi Corridor. Located in Gansu Province, it begins in the east in Wushao Mountain. To the north is the desolated Heli Mountain, Longshou Mountain, and the Tengger and Badain Jaran deserts; to the south are the snow-covered Qilian Mountains. The 'corridor' extends about a thousand kilometres in length and a hundred kilometres in width. As a result of its long and narrow shape stretching from northwest to southeast, and its location west of the Yellow River, it got its the name 'Hexi Corridor' (*hexi* in Chinese means west of the river).

The Hexi Corridor

Since entering the Hexi Corridor, I encountered multiple sandstorms and instances of extremely high temperatures.

On 17 August, a sudden gust of wind blacked out the sky with sand, reducing visibility to less than ten metres. Walking one kilometre was more difficult than ten kilometres on a regular day. When I finally got close to Shuangta Reservoir located midstream of the Shule River, it was already dark. Luckily, I spotted a small restaurant by the side of the road, so I decided to call it a day and rest there.

I did not have much cash left, so I decided to see if I could spend some money on food and in return sleep in an empty room next to the restaurant for free. I showed the owner my ID and explained my situation, but he didn't budge.

"You can eat if you pay," he said blankly, "but don't even think about staying here for nothing."

No matter what I said, he wouldn't change his mind. Becoming increasingly impatient, he said: "If you're not planning to eat here, please leave. You're affecting my business."

I figured that I had to buy some food at the very least, so I asked one last time: "How much is the cheapest dish?"

Frustrated at the ridiculously high prices and the indifference of the owner, I left without another word.

Under a dark sky and a gathering strong sandstorm, I could barely move after struggling to walk another few miles. Surrounding me was a vast desert without any shelter, but the sandstorm prevented me from erecting my tent. Exhausted, I paused on a sand dune, covered my head with clothes, and lowered my body to the ground. I didn't choose a low-lying area because, even though it would provide better shelter, the accumulation of sand could easily bury a person. I ate a few mouthfuls of Xinjiang naan bread with some water and swallowed without chewing. Because at that point, I wasn't sure if I was eating food or sand.

That night I didn't sleep, fearing I might not be able to wake up again. Overwhelmed, anxious, trapped… bitterness came to mind, but I told myself to stay strong.

Every couple of hours, my entire body was covered with sand. I had to stay alert all night to shake off the sand and avoid getting buried alive. But even so, fine sand would quietly enter my nose, ears and mouth, making it difficult to breathe.

After an entire night of struggle, morning came and the sandstorm died down. I stood up and dug into my ears and nostrils; the sand inside had already turned to mud balls. I rinsed my nose with water, tried to raise my spirits and continued my journey.

Saving wildlife

On 21 November, I was nearing Yuling, Shaanxi Province. This would be my third time in Shaanxi.

At about noon, when I found a shelter in the wilderness to rest, a hare suddenly ran passed me. The moment before it should have disappeared from sight, it jumped on the spot a few times, apparently hindered by something.

I immediately went up and followed it. A dozen metres away, the hare was struggling hard with a wire looped around its neck. It took me a lot of work to finally untie the steel wire, but it was already too late.

Those who set the trap would come back a few days later to collect the animal and would then set up new ones. I had seen many traps during my journey; some with steel wire, some iron clamps and others huge nets. It was not in my power to determine what people do to wildlife, but at least I could protect those I did find.

A few years ago, I was in a mountainous area in Guizhou Province. While passing by a landslide caused by heavy rain, I saw a bird's nest tumble down to the middle of the road. Inside the nest were newly hatched chicks. As the landslide continued, mud and stones kept falling, leaving the chicks in great danger. They seemed to know it too; they kept on twittering and chirping. Their mother, on the other hand, was desperately spiralling around in the air and anxiously landing on the ground from time to time, but it could not move the hatchlings to a safe place.

I quickly put down my pack, took off my hat and rushed up to the muddy road. As I was putting the birds in my hat one after another, the mother bird let out a bitter and dismal cry and dived down several times, trying to attack my head. It must have thought I was trying to take away her chicks.

The cry of grief pierced my heart.

Holding the hat with great care, I climbed to a safe place and then put the birds on the grass. Immediately, the mother bird attempted to land and approach the little birds. As I was leaving, the mother bird flew over my head. It circled for several laps while seeming to cheer over and over, and finally it flew away.

It was such a delightful experience. Perhaps gratitude is not just a human quality, but rather something that is shared by all creatures.

Various animals encountered on my journey

A pair of cranes bellowing out a song

Little ducklings enjoying the warmth of a springtime river

A lamb suckling on its mother's milk

A loving mother monkey

2004
HOMEWARD JOURNEY

This autumn, I missed my home town more than ever.

This friendship I will treasure during my entire trip and cherish all my life.

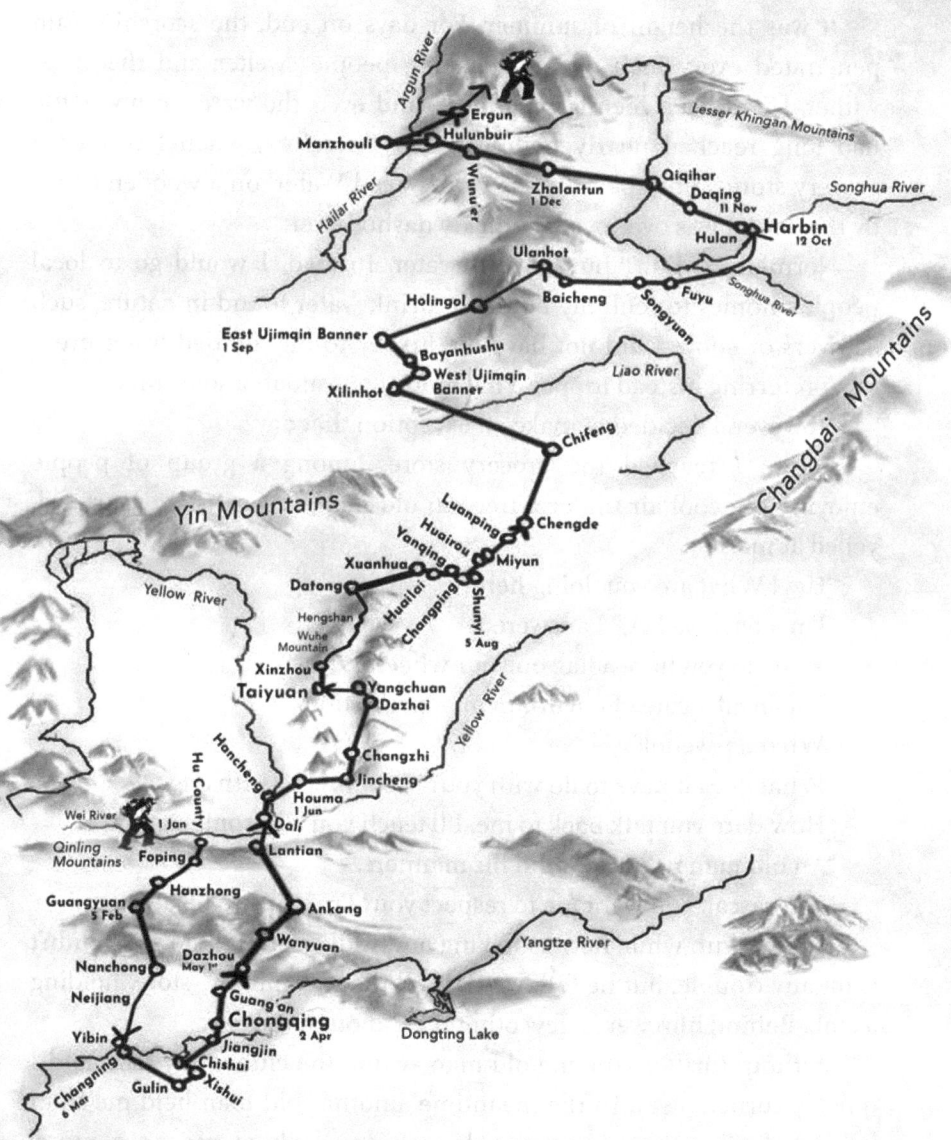

An inexplicable humiliation

I arrived in Xidi Village, Luanping County, Hebei Province on the afternoon of 9 August 2004.

It was the height of summer. For days on end, the scorching sun penetrated every inch of land, making people swelter and the crops wither. I had been feeling breathless, and even the water in my bottle had long reached nearly boiling point. Therefore, when I spotted a grocery store, and especially the words 'Iced Water' on a wooden board by the door, I was overjoyed. I quickly dashed over.

Normally I didn't buy bottled water. Instead, I would go to local people's homes to refill my bottle, or drink water found in nature, such as rivers or snow. I did not have the luxury to buy bottled water every day, preferring instead to spend my money on valuable souvenirs.

However, I decided to make an exception that day.

Before I reached the grocery store, among a group of people enjoying the cool air under a tree, an old man, at least sixty years old, yelled at me.

"Hey! What are you doing here?"

"I'm a backpacker," I answered.

"Why do you have a flag on your wheelbarrow?"

"I'm an advocate of environmental protection."

"What a psycho!"

"What does it have to do with you?" I countered with anger.

"How dare you talk back to me. I'll teach you a lesson!"

"An old man needs to mind his manners."

"You rascal. You want me to respect you? I'm going to beat you up!"

He stood up while he was talking and walked straight to me. I didn't want any trouble, but he followed me all the way into the store, holding a club. Behind him were a few other men about his age.

Without further ado, the old man swung the club at my face, and I quickly turned away. In the meantime, another old man held me from behind, letting the angry man launch the club at me once more. Furious, I almost fought back, yet thinking of the trouble I may cause to them and to my plan, I held back.

As I dodged time after time, the club accidentally landed on an old man behind me. He grimaced in pain and instantly released me. I took the opportunity to jump out of the store; however, they immediately went after me again.

I picked up my camera, hoping to capture their ugly faces, yet they frantically rushed up to grab it from me. Circles and circles of people came to watch the scene, yet no one came forward to help. As I was dodging, I called the police. I thought, if the police came, they would surely be taught a lesson.

A female operator picked up the phone. After I briefly explained the situation, she said: "Be at ease. We'll be there shortly."

Seeing that I had called the police, the old men became timid. Holding the clubs angrily, they stared at me without moving. I sat silently next to my wheelbarrow, waiting for the police to arrive. Yet half an hour passed, and the police were still nowhere to be seen. The old men became more and more restless. I knew I couldn't afford to wait any longer, so I quietly pushed my old pal and quickly left the village.

I didn't slow down until I arrived at a place where no one was around. My mouth was parched, my tongue scorched and my heart was pounding. I was only trying to buy a bottle of iced water – how come I had to endure such humiliation?

In fact, over the years, I was subjected to countless insults, abuse and sometimes even assaults. As much as I tried to stay strong, I would sometimes shed tears or feel unjustly treated. Eventually, though, I always reminded myself of my goal to walk across China. It was because of the dream I held so passionately that I was able to turn every setback and tribulation into a new motive that encouraged me to march forward.

'Working' eighteen hours a day

In late August, I entered the Inner Mongolian Plateau.

The savannah stretched as far as the eye could see, and the yellow hills in the distance gently rolled as wide as the horizon itself. Walking in such a beautiful landscape broadens the mind and enables one to leave all troubles behind.

Sparsely populated, this land only had the occasional *oboos*, sacred stone heaps according to Mongolian folk religion. The colourful prayer flags on the *oboos* fluttered in the wind, as if welcoming guests from afar. Herds of cattle and flocks of sheep were feeding on the grassland, enjoying the selfless gift of nature.

Walking with the wheelbarrow, I would lay on the grass from time to time to rest. The grassland was abundant with little white flowers that I could not name. Fine and brilliant, they extended from my feet in all directions. In the distance, the frequent cries of larks could be heard; one sound louder than the other, one more profound than the other.

For a while, I switched between lying down and sitting up, enjoying the wonder of nature. I felt at one with nature; there was no more to seek, but so much to receive. Beneath the vast infinite blue, my thoughts drifted to the distant horizon with the white clouds. Not the least trace of the hardships and humiliation that I once felt remained.

At 4am on 1 September, I departed West Ujimqin Banner to proceed to East Ujimqin Banner.

I didn't realise the time until the morning sunshine had completely covered the prairie, casting warmth upon me. The weather was unusually pleasant since I stepped onto the plateau. With my spirits raised, every step seemed to be more brisk and lively.

At noon, a strong breeze started blowing. I had been walking for quite a while, yet I still couldn't seem to find any sign of human beings.

Finally, after a few hours, I went up to a hillock and spotted a small town in the distance. I was ravished with joy at the prospect of being able to recharge my body; yet, after another three hours of walking, I realised that even though the town looked close, it was in fact still far away. The flat and endless grassland lacked any sort of reference point, which resulted in my misjudgment and premature celebration.

The sun was already setting, and all I could do was to keep walking in the dark night. At 10pm, I arrived at a hostel in East Ujimqin. Most people had already gone to bed, and the restaurants were all closed. I bought a pack of instant noodles for dinner, threw myself onto the bed, and instantly fell asleep.

That day I had walked for eighteen hours, travelling about eighty-six kilometres. I had covered more ground than on any other day in the entire ten-year journey.

Returning to my home town

In mid-September, after leaving the Inner Mongolian Plateau, I passed through Jilin Province and entered Heilongjiang Province. On the south bank of the Songhua River were a few aspen trees whose leaves had already turned golden yellow. Occasionally, I spotted some ponds amid the grass, which was typical of northeast China. I was getting closer and closer to my home town.

Wild geese were flying in formation, heading south. For me, my home in the north was where my heart belonged.

In the twinkling of an eye, I had been away from home for six years. During this time, my sister and brother-in-law had frequently travelled to the post office to collect my parcels regardless of the weather; they had spent a large amount of time and effort keeping the items I'd collected in good condition; they had always been supportive of my trip and concerned about my safety. My gratitude to them was immense. Our deep concern and care for one another over the phone was about to turn into a physical reunion. How could I not be thrilled?

At the end of 1999, I did get the opportunity to go back to my home town. But since I was busy getting all sorts of documents ready for Hong Kong and Macau, I couldn't spend enough time with my family, nor was I able to visit my parents' grave. This time, I was set to fulfil my wish.

The frost in the northeast comes early. The leaves on the trees had begun to fall and the ground was covered in a bright gold colour. Most of the summer birds had flown away, leaving only the wild pigeons to forage in the newly harvested soybean and corn fields.

Those sounds were an indication of an excellent harvest, and those images were reminiscent of childhood playfulness.

On 15 October, I reached Hulan and arrived at my sister's home. At the front door, we hugged each other tightly. Holding my hands as if I might run away at any moment, my sister kept on asking me all sorts of questions. As we talked, I noticed the deepened wrinkles on her face and the grey flecks in her hair. I felt pain in my heart.

A while later, I visited my parents' grave.

During the previous six years of backpacking, I had many near-death experiences. My parents would have been greatly saddened if I hadn't made it back. Thinking about it now, I let out all the bitterness and grievances that I had been carrying with me throughout these years, and I burst into tears.

After calming down, I added some fresh soil to my parents' grave and touched my head to the ground three times. I secretly vowed to return four years later to worship my parents again.

As the sun started to set, I walked along the Hulan River. The cool wind stroked my cheeks as gently as my mother used to do. During six years of wandering, I had always been very careful, as if treading on thin ice. At this moment, however, I was able to be fully relax. The familiar roads, friends and family made me feel incomparably secure and warm. It was at this point that I fully appreciated the meaning and significance of home.

On the way home, I passed through areas of wasteland where the crows flew from the top of one tree to another. Waves of smoke were rising from the village; families had begun to cook dinner.

My sister was waiting for me when I got back. Having someone to wait for you is a blessing. But I didn't dare cling to this feeling. After a short reunion with my family and friends, I picked up my pack and hurried again onto the road.

Reed marshes

In mid-November, after passing Daqing, I arrived in Zhalong Nature Reserve, the home of the red-crowned crane.

The wetland reserve consists of large swamps and countless small lakes. The reeds swaying in the wind are such a delightful scene in early winter. Large flocks of red-crowned cranes come here during April and May to shelter and mate. They would later continue their migration north to Russia.

In the afternoon, I passed a village called Kenhe and entered the beautiful reed marshes of Zhalong Nature Reserve. Ahead of me was a boundless stretch of withered reed and a reed pond that seemed to be frozen over. Unable to hold my curiosity, I asked a woman passing by if the ice was sturdy enough to walk on. She told me that it should be fine, but I had to be extra careful. She kindly gave me a long stick with which to probe the ice. After determining my path, I stepped on the ice, which occasionally creaked as I took my steps.

Zhalong Nature Reserve

After walking for some time, the sun had started to set, shining its hue onto the reeds. Before I knew it, I found myself walking on ice in a field of golden reeds.

Suddenly, a cracking sound came from under my feet. I realised I had been stepping on a particularly thin section. The ice broke, and I plunged into the water below. The water was not deep, yet my pack prevented me from grabbing on to anything. I quickly took it off and slid it away from me, hoping I could then grab onto some reeds or ice nearby. Unfortunately, the ice continued to break around me.

I found my feet sinking into the soft mud. If I couldn't think of a way to get myself out of the water; I would soon sink deeper and deeper until I was completely swallowed.

I then decided to move my body forward as much as possible. Focusing on a thicker layer of ice, I sprawled onto it and was able to get my whole body out of the water. I spent all my remaining energy on crawling a few metres forward before I finally stood up slowly on a thicker patch of ice.

My drenched clothes soon became stiff from the cold. I shivered in the chilly wind. Fortunately, the spare clothes in my pack were kept dry by a plastic bag.

I quickly changed, took up my pack and went on. It wasn't long before I heard a rustling sound nearby. I stopped and listened carefully; it sounded like footsteps.

I was overjoyed to find another person. I followed where the sound came from and shouted a few times: "Hello?" In the dense reed marshes, the visibility was only three to four metres.

"Who is it?" the person responded.

"I'm a backpacker. Do you know how far Zhalong Nature Reserve is from here?"

"Come over here. I'll show you the way."

It turned out that there were two people, both reed marsh wardens. With their help, I successfully made it through the frozen lake.

That night, I found myself back in the loose mud, bogged down deeper and deeper. I wanted to cry out for help, yet I couldn't make a sound. Waking up from this nightmare, I was still clutching my pillow.

Brothers reunited

In early December, I entered Inner Mongolia for the second time. I took a special trip to Wunuer Town to visit my second eldest brother.

My brother had moved there about a decade ago. He used to run a small business and had borrowed some money from me, but we had been out of contact since then.

The gate of his house was left unlatched. I knocked on the door a few times, but no one answered, so I pushed it open and shouted: "Brother!"

The door opened and a thin, tanned man with a slightly bent back walked out. "Brother!" I could hardly recognise him. He had grown so much older.

A multitude of feelings surged up on seeing him again after so many years; yet he stared at me blankly and hesitated for a while before he uttered: "Third brother?"

"No, it's your fourth brother, Fuzi."

His eyes lit up. "Oh it's you, Fuzi! My eyes are getting worse. I'm so sorry I didn't recognise you," he said, while leading me into the room.

"Where's my sister-in-law?" I asked.

"She's working in the field. Your niece is at school."

My brother, even after so many years, was still a person of few words. I asked him about his health and advised him to go to a decent hospital, but he said he was not seriously ill and that he'd be fine after taking some medicine. After a short silence, he said softly: "Little brother, you must have suffered a lot these years travelling. I really wanted to return your money, but…"

"Big brother," I hurried to say, "don't worry about that. Just please take care of yourself."

He began to shed tears. "You sit down and drink some water. I'll pick up your niece. After your sister-in-law comes back, let's have dinner together at home."

"A friend has already arranged meals and accommodation for me. No need to go to the trouble. Let's go pick up the child together."

At the school gate, a teenage girl hopped in front of us. My brother said that she was my niece.

She looked at me curiously and finally called me 'Uncle'. I gave her a hug and then tucked into her hand a few hundred yuan that I'd put aside beforehand. My brother, though, would not let her take it.

"Fuzi, you'll need to use this money on your trip. I'm sorry that I failed to help you."

"Please take the money. It's for my niece to go to school."

That night I didn't go back to my brother's place because I had to leave early the next morning.

The ninth day after Chinese New Year in 2007, I received a phone call from home. My brother had died from sickness. I grieved for a very long time. Who would have thought that our brief reunion that day would be the last time I would ever see him?

Dragging the sledge

From hell to heaven

On 18 December, I strode on Hulun Buir Grassland like a wild wolf. The average temperature was minus 35 degrees Celsius.

Before exposing myself to such extreme weather, I made some careful preparations. First, I bought of pair of size 46 cotton and rubber shoes. Those shoes were three sizes larger than what I would normally wear, since they enabled me to put on a pair of felt socks and woollen stockings. I kept my hands warm and agile with a pair of mittens a friend had given me that were made of wool and cotton. Having by this time got rid of my wheelbarrow, I also ordered a sledge, on which I put all my bags. Pulling the bags instead of carrying them saved me a lot of energy.

The winter storm was even more severe in the wilderness. My face was frozen, but at least the rest of my body felt decently warm from all the preparations I had taken. The hardest part of the day was when it was its coldest. In order to keep my mind from going blank, I had to occasionally rub snow on my face.

At about dusk, I saw a small railway station in Wugunuoer. Because walking long distances heated up my body at a time when the outside temperature was extremely low, the sweat that collected at the bottom of my trousers now became frozen. I checked the surroundings and didn't find any restaurants or inns, so I tried my luck at the station.

I asked the stationmaster if I could spend the night on a bench in the waiting room, but he wasn't an easy person. The stove burning hot, my frozen cotton trousers began to drip water.

Seeing that I did not move an inch, he started to show impatience and pushed me towards the door ferociously. I begged him yet again. "Please. I have nowhere to go. I could freeze to death tonight!"

Little did I think that he would reject me without blinking. "It's none of my business."

Before I could say another word, he slammed the door shut.

At that moment, the weather outside was cold, but my heart was colder.

There was no other choice but to keep walking. I knocked on many families' doors, yet no one would take me in.

I thought, perhaps I could find a herdsman's flock of sheep and sleep with them to keep myself warm when it got darker. When I thought better of it, I realised that I could end up being beaten if the herdsman took me for a thief.

As I was lost in thought, I noticed a farm vehicle. Someone was trying to heat up the water tank with fire. I went forward and greeted him: "Hi there! I'm a backpacker. Do you know a place where I could stay for the night? I can pay any price!"

He responded without lifting his head. "Help me jump-start the car first."

I saw hope from his reaction, so I hurried to help. The engine finally started. "I can send you to Weibo Station," he said. "I'm Zhang and I'm in charge of that station."

I hesitated. "That's still pretty far from here. Do you know anyone in Wugunuoer Village?"

"I'll try."

It was less than five minutes before we arrived at a farm house. I set aside the sledge and followed him into the room. The sky was already completely dark. The house was filled with steam from cooking, and I couldn't see anyone clearly without standing right up close.

"Hey brother!" Zhang called. "I've brought back a friend."

"Come on in," someone answered inside.

The family were making dumplings. I told them my situation, and they gladly accepted me.

"Don't worry about the money. Please put down your kid first."

I chuckled and said: "Actually, it's my backpack, not a child."

I handed him my documents, but he didn't look at them.

"Xiangmin never went to school before and he can't even write his own name," Zhang explained. "However, he's an especially kind person. Let's have some drinks first to warm up the body."

"Dear, please make more dumplings," Xiangmin said to a woman inside the room.

Within a few moments, the steaming dumplings were served at the table. Xiangmin took out a bottle of Inner Mongolia alcohol from a plastic bag and filled everyone's glass. It was such a blessing to be able to have a drink and to eat hot dumplings in the freezing weather.

My trousers began to drip again from the heat. Xiangmin chuckled at the sight and took me to a side room to change into his cotton padded coat and trousers. He also asked his wife to add fuel to the fire and hang my clothes to dry. His warm hospitality reminded me of my eldest brother at home.

That night, I was lying in a warm bed but couldn't manage to fall asleep. Within just a few hours, I had experienced both hell and heaven, and had a taste of the fickleness of human nature.

Early next morning, Xiangmin cooked me breakfast. Before

departure, he said to me: "Lei, I have a small request. Can I take a photo with you?"

"Of course!" I set up the tripod and called his wife to join us for a photo.

I treasured this friendship throughout my trip and will do so all my life.

Eating dumplings at Xiangmin's home

2005
MY HEART, FARTHEST AWAY

The furthest points I reached on my journey were Tianya Haijiao in Hainan Province in the south, Jigen Village, Wuqia County, Xinjiang in the west, Arctic Village in Mohe County in the north, and Wusu Town in the east.

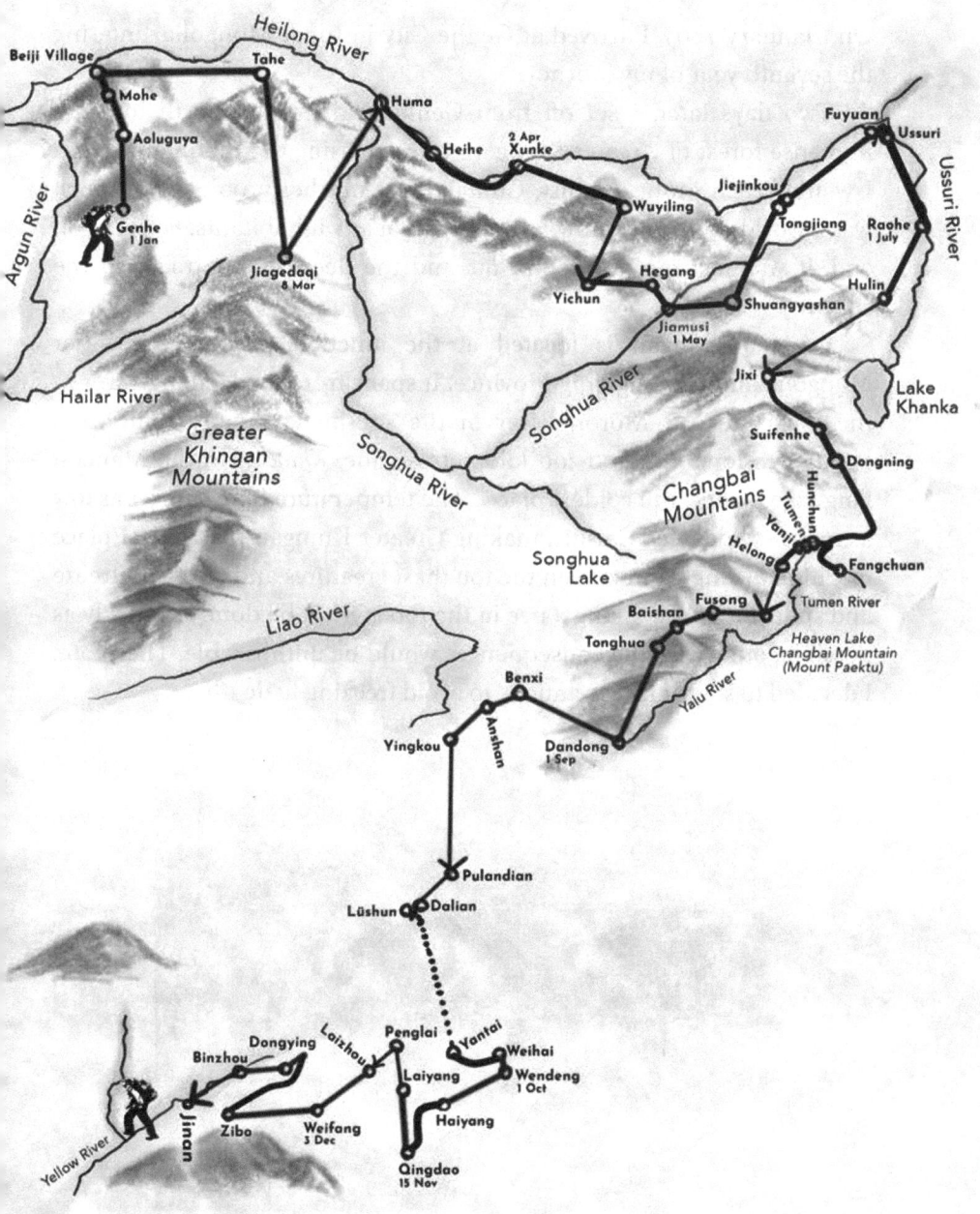

From Greater Khingan to Arctic Village

On 1 January 2005, I arrived at Genhe City in Inner Mongolia, entering the seventh year of my journey.

Two days later, I set off from Genhe and headed north into the immense forest of Greater Khingan. After crossing the mountain range, I would reach Mohe County, China's most northerly point. The forest was a world of ice and snow, with no sign of any inhabitants. For days on end, it was just me, my footprints and the deep sledge tracks in the snow.

Greater Khingan is located at the junction of northern Inner Mongolia and Heilongjiang Province. It spans from the Heilong River in the north, to Xar Moron River in the south. It is more than 1,200 kilometres long and 200-300 kilometres wide. *Khingan* in the Manchu language means 'the coldest place'. The temperature here can get as low as minus 52 degrees Celsius, making Greater Khingan the coldest place in China during winter. Even the toughest creatures and trees can freeze and split. Tasks like taking a pee in the forest must be done as quickly as possible; otherwise the consequences would be unthinkable. Therefore, I decided to stay at forest stations to avoid freezing to death.

Braving the cold weather

Nights in Greater Khingan were particularly long. Ever since I walked onto the mountain range, I would get up before dawn and immediately begin my day's journey after a simple breakfast. Only then could I reach the next boarding point before dark. The weather was normally the coldest between 4am and 6am. I had to maintain a fast pace to prevent my limbs from feeling numb and my face from experiencing the pricking pain from the cold.

Every day, I walked on through the deep forest with snow on my hat and frost in my beard. The weather was so extreme that I was constantly challenging the limits of my body.

However, the cold is more bearable than loneliness. Daxing'anling Prefecture has a tiny population, so I never saw anyone in person. Occasionally, I might spot a few large trucks loaded with timber passing through. I was fortunate enough to receive the occasional text message from friends asking my whereabouts. Their warm greetings and encouragement helped me through the rough winter.

On the afternoon of 18 January, I reached the far north of China, Arctic Village, Mohe County. Having conquered the bitter cold weather over the previous weeks, I felt a great sense of satisfaction. As tired as I was, I sped up to reach the post office to get a precious postmark.

Having left the post office, I walked straight to the Heilong River without stopping to take in the beautiful scenery. In front of the 'Shenzhou North Pole' stone tablet, I set up my tripod, took out the Chinese flag and captured the moment that would be forever precious to me.

I stood on the river bank and looked across at the villages in Russia. They were so mysterious and serene in the afterglow of the sunset, emitting an almost cordial feeling. In fact, our Chinese ancestors had resided on the other side of the river a century ago. On impulse, I raised the Chinese flag over my head and waved to the distance.

With mixed feelings, I started walking towards the centre of the river. Due to the heavily accumulation of snow in the river, border soldiers had used a sledge to draw a line down the centre of the river to signify the borderline between the two countries. On that line, I stripped down to my bare chest and sat down to meditate and to quietly perceive the tenacity of life.

On 17 January, I left Arctic Village and went down south. Three days later, in the afternoon, I arrived in Tuqiang Town, Mohe County, where I had met Yu Chunshun for the first time in the summer of 1989. How time flies. In the twinkling of an eye, sixteen years had passed. His spirit, however, had continued to influence and motivate me on my journey.

The morning light in Arctic Village

Meditating in the centre of the Heilong River

The place where the sun rises first

At dawn on 11 May, I arrived at the Three Rivers Junction (Sanjiangkou), where the Songhua and Heilong rivers meet four kilometres northeast of Tongjiang. Russia is on the north bank.

The natural wonders of Sanjiangkou

Along the way, I paid a few visits to the fishermen who lived in the lower reaches of the Songhua. They all said that the number of fish in the river had been falling due to pollution. By contrast, the water in the Heilong was still considered clean.

On the afternoon of the second day, I arrived in a village in Tongjiang inhabited by people from the Hezhe ethnic minority. The Hezhe are mainly found in three counties in Heilongjiang: Tongjiang, Raohe and Wuyuan. They are the only nationality in northern China who live by fishing. They have their own spoken language, which does not have written characters. While the older people can still converse in Hezhe, most of the younger generation can't, leading to fears that the language will gradually disappear.

The Hezhes live on a land that has been ideal for fishing and hunting through the ages. Years ago, people used the phrase 'hunting with a bat, fishing with a ladle and cooking with a chicken that flies to your pot' to describe the abundance of resources on their land.

I came across a couple by the river who were approaching their seventies. I learned that when they were young, they had caught Chinese sturgeon as heavy as 500 kilograms in the Heilong and Ussuri rivers; however, the government later prohibited civilians from fishing for sturgeon.

A fish skin costume of the Hezhe

The Hezhes used to wear some very distinctive shoes and clothing made from fish skin. But ever since fishing was banned, such clothing could only be sold as handicrafts for extremely high prices, up to tens of thousands of yuan.

This reminds me of the exquisite handicrafts made from birch bark by the Oroqen people. Great Khingan is covered in birch trees, meaning birch bark is very accessible; however, because young people are unwilling to learn the traditional craft, it's in danger of dying out just like those fish skin costumes. The gradual disappearance of these ethnic arts and crafts is heart-wrenching.

On 15 May, I passed Yinchuan Village, Tongjiang County and entered Fuyuan, the easternmost county of China. After hurrying to the post office to get a postmark, I arrived at 5pm at the 'first sentry post of the east', Wusu Town, where the Wusuli River merges with the Heilong.

Birch bark handicrafts made by the Oroqen

At 3am the next day, I walked to the river to watch the sunrise, the first place in China to witness daybreak. When I arrived, the wide river was already bathed in the bright rosy dawn. At 3.26am, the sun emerged from the river like an enormous fireball. I was lucky to be able to witness this scene because, according to locals, it had been two months since they had seen a cloudless sky.

At this point, I completed the visit to the four endpoints of China.

The four endpoints: the southern monument at Tianya Haijiao

The four endpoints: the western boundary monument in Erkeshtam

The four endpoints: Arctic Village in Mohe County

The four endpoints: the eastern boundary monument in Yinchuan

On 25 March 2000, I reached the most southerly point in China, Tianya Haijiao in Hainan Province; on 14 September 2002, I went to the most westerly point, the border between China and Kyrgyzstan in Jigen Village, Wuqia County, Xinjiang, where I watched China's last dusk of the day; on 14 January 2005, I arrived in Arctic Village in Mohe County, Heilongjiang Province, where the temperature was below minus 50 degrees Celsius; and today, at this moment, I stood at the easternmost point in China, witnessing the first sunshine of the day.

A special birthday

On 11 December, I came to Dongying in the province of Shandong, travel-worn and weary. My biggest wish during this part of the trip was to witness the spectacular scene of the Yellow River's entry into the sea.

The Yellow River is the mother river of the Chinese nation. For thousands of years, she has given birth to the ancient and splendid Chinese civilisation and nurtured tens of thousands of sons and daughters with her selfless mind. At the end of every journey, however, she unreservedly dedicates herself to the vast ocean.

Back in March 2002, I had the opportunity to see the mother river for the first time when I was walking along the ancient Tangbo Road from Xining, Qinghai Province, to Changdu, Tibet. There, I walked over the so-called 'first bridge on the upper reaches of the Yellow River'. The water at this point is quite different to the public imagination of what the Yellow River looks like; it was crystal clear. I scooped up a mouthful of water and was delighted to taste its sweetness.

Four years later, I came to the river mouth a thousand miles away. For most of the year, ferries carry passengers from one bank to the other; during winter, however, ice forms in the river channel drift quickly downstream, preventing single boats from sailing on the river. The only way to pass through is to connect several vessels together with wire rope to create a strong foundation.

On this winter morning, the sun shone onto the Yellow River, which was partly covered with ice, making the surface glitter and sparkle. I boarded a ferry on the south bank. As the ferry moved forward, I could hear the 'click click' sound of the hull scraping the ice. Later, when the ferry reached the middle of the river, I stood on the bow and looked into the distance where the river met the sea. The Yellow River rushed continuously into the Bo Sea like thousands of horses and soldiers; further away, where the two joined, the muddy yellow and clear blue water distinguished themselves from each other, creating a wondrous sight.

Later that day, I stayed in Hekou District, where the Shengli oil field is located. The next day, a few young fellows from the oil field invited me to speak to their company.

The audience were very enthusiastic about learning what had happened to me on my journey. There was one question, however, that left the deepest impression. Someone asked me how I celebrated holidays, especially my birthday. I confessed to them that all these years, except occasionally when I got invited to events, I never really celebrated my birthday. Perhaps there were moments when the idea of treating myself a little during public holidays came to mind, but the ultimate goal of finishing the trip always persuaded me to set aside everything else.

After eating with them, I embarked again on my long journey. A few days later, when I was on my way to Jinan, I received a call from them.

"Lei, today is your birthday, right? We remembered from our last conversation. Would you mind if we came celebrate it with you?"

I had never done anything special on my birthday for these past years on the road; and yet my new-found friends wanted to celebrate it with me. I didn't know how to express sufficient gratitude towards them.

Late at night, they drove to the small inn I was staying at and brought me a birthday cake and drinks. The cake candles having been lit, they surrounded me and sang happy birthday. I secretly shed tears of joy. We exchanged our views on life and our dreams; we laughed and cried. That night, we drank to our hearts' content.

Time hurries like flowing water. Within the blink of an eye, years have passed. Whenever it's my birthday, I always think of this beautiful memory. I sincerely thank every friend I've had the opportunity to meet and wish them a happy and healthy life.

The Yellow River

2006
WALKING TO PURITY

———

Eight years of travelling has changed me. I have become more genuine and true to myself.

By taking the road less travelled, I have witnessed endless beautiful scenery and experienced countless wonders.

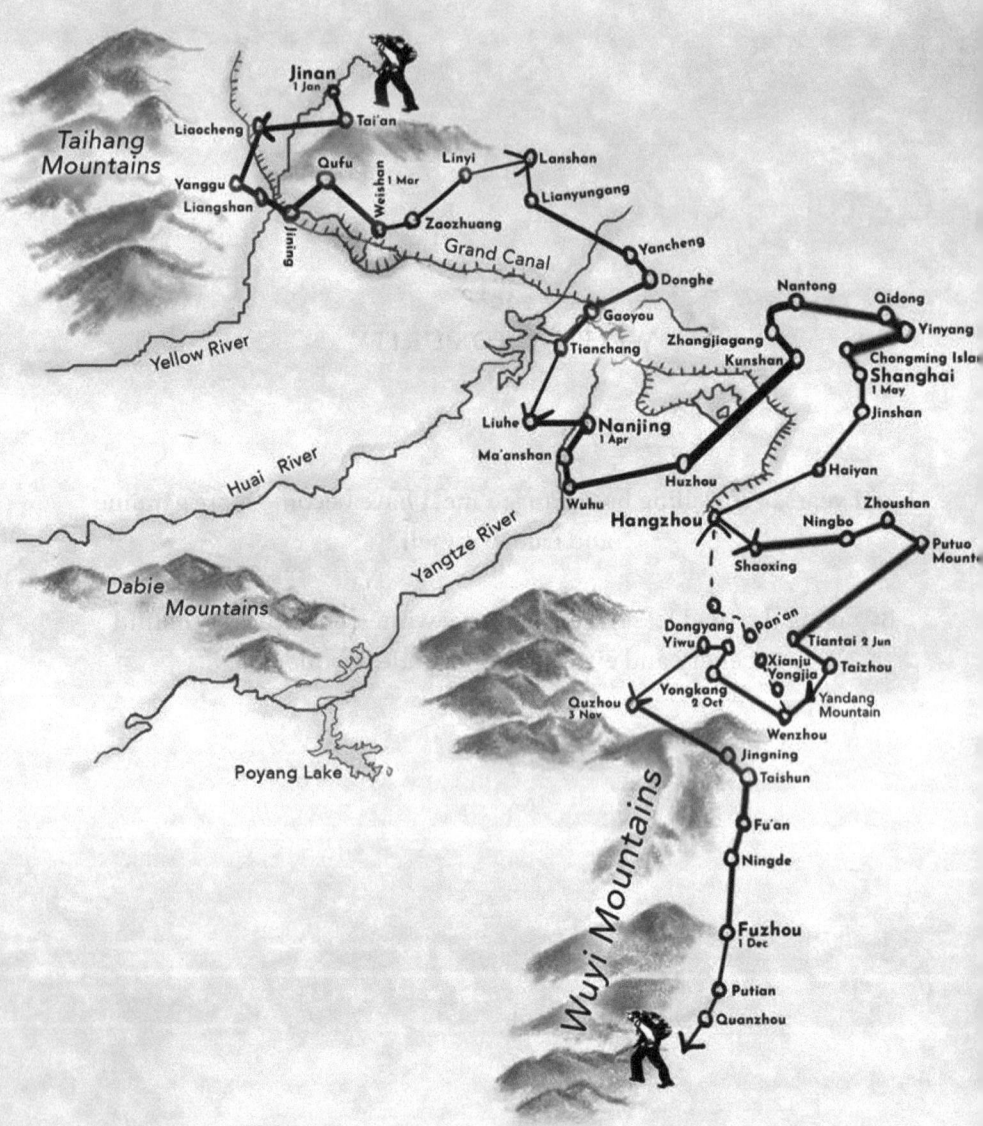

Entering the ivory tower

On 29 March 2006, I entered Jiangsu Province for the second time.

From Tianchang to Luhe District, I arrived at Nanjing for the second time. The first time was in 1999 when I passed the city from west to east; on this occasion I came from the north and was heading south.

As I approached Nanjing Hongshan Forest Zoo, Lu Di and Mai Zi from the Environmental Council of Nanjing University of Information Science and Technology reached out to me, hoping I might give a lecture to their students about my hiking experience and the concept of environmental protection. I gladly accepted the invitation.

On the second day, when I arrived at the university, a large crowd had already gathered at the gate, including students from several other colleges nearby. Seeing this scene from afar, I began to feel somewhat nervous. After all, I didn't even graduate from primary school, and now I was about to give a speech to college students. Could I really handle it? I convinced myself that I should treat the speech as a conversation with friends, since what could be more natural than sharing my life experience and inner thoughts and feelings?

The result exceeded my expectations. The students not only responded enthusiastically to my presentation, but also expressed interest in the idea of backpacking.

At lunchtime, I handed out ten pairs of chopsticks, which I had prepared in advance, since I am against disposable ones on environmental grounds. I was pleased to find that many students had already brought their own chopsticks.

Though the event didn't last long, I was lucky to make a few friends in the process. Constantly travelling on the road prevented me from talking to them face to face; however, in the coming days we were able to speak on mobile phones to exchange ideas, share our views on life and build deeper relationships.

A student majoring in meteorology appreciated the importance of weather during my trip, so he texted me daily to give me the forecast in places I would reach the next day. He stuck to this habit for over a year until he graduated from college. His texts helped me greatly in arranging my trips. Another student was worried that I might get lonely during my journey, so he always texted or called to encourage me. Some students who were about to graduate consulted me about their plans after college, while others asked me about romantic relationships, sometimes confiding in me about their love lives. They saw me as an older brother and sometimes trusted me more than their parents.

Responding to their trust, I wholeheartedly listened to what they had to say and offered my input. Those conversations and communications also enriched my spiritual being. The students were full of curiosity about my life in nature, while for my part, I yearned for the college life that they were experiencing.

A heartfelt conversation

In Nanjing, I met my old friend Jin Sheng. We got acquainted back in 2004 in Shanxi Province. Noticing how frequently I wore out my shoes, he had given me several pairs of nice trainers. This time, he arranged accommodation for me and gave me another pair of new shoes and a digital camera. That was the first time I got to use a digital camera since I started backpacking.

A local reporter interviewed me during dinner and another friend recorded the interview. Perhaps this could sum up my journey so far.

Q: What's the biggest change you see in yourself after these eight years?

A: The biggest change is probably my mentality. Eight years of travelling has made me more genuine and true to myself. For example, in the past I was ashamed of the fact that I only received an elementary school education and that I had to depend on others financially because my parents died when I was very young. But now these facts no longer bother me, and I allow myself to be vulnerable in front of people.

Q: Can you tell me what you've learned from your backpacking experience?

A: Compared with nature, human beings seem so insignificant. When I was crossing the Taklamakan Desert, I felt smaller than an ant. I always had the mindset to conquer nature; yet, later I gradually realised that people had to respect and follow the laws of nature.

Q: How heavy is your pack? What's your average daily walking distance? What's the farthest you've walked during a day?

A: In the beginning, my pack weighed 45 kilograms; now I have reduced it to 25 to 30 kilograms. I cover on average 40 kilometres a day and the farthest I've walked in a single day was 86 kilometres when I was passing the Inner Mongolia grassland.

Q: Have you ever thought about giving up?

A: I can't say I have never had this thought. But every time I think about it, I also think about the advance preparations I made – it was ten years of training and groundwork. I couldn't just give up when things got a little difficult.

Q: Have any of your hardships been unbearable?

A: Yes, I have experienced difficult times but there have also been moments of great joy. By taking the road less travelled, I have witnessed endless beautiful scenery and experienced countless wonders. Sometimes, when waking up in the wild, I heard birds chirping and smelled the fragrance of flowers and trees. I couldn't ask for anything more wonderful than that. One time in Tibet, I looked up to the sky and saw stars that appeared so close that I thought I could grab them.

Q: What's been your primary source for learning field survival skills?

A: I read a lot of books about field survival training in Western armies but didn't find them very useful. In comparison, the experiences I've accumulated throughout the years and methods that I came up with myself have worked better. For example, once I got surrounded by a pack of wolves. At this moment of life and death, I survived by lighting firecrackers, spraying pesticide and burning clothes. My experience told me that almost all animals are afraid of fire, which was why I thought about burning my clothes to drive away the wolves.

Q: What were your lowest and highest points?

A: When I was tired and hungry, I got rejected and sometimes even beaten up in grocery stores or lodging places because people thought I was crazy. Those were the times when I felt the most wronged and bitter. More often, though, countless kind people have helped me selflessly, and I was often moved to tears.

Q: Has the support from your friends been more like a motivation or pressure for you?

A: From the very beginning, I didn't feel much pressure because I simply wanted to realise my dream. Recently, however, I have felt more responsibility on my shoulders, so I feel I must keep going until I finish this ten-year journey.

Cherish the source of life

On 24 April, after a day-long journey, I arrived at Yuantuojiao Scenic Area in Jiangsu Province, the estuary of the Yangtze River.

It was drizzling early the next morning. I got on to a private boat to leave for Chongming Island.

Chongming is located at the mouth of the Yangtze. It is the third largest island in China and is said to be the largest estuary island in the world formed by the accumulation of sand or sediment. Known as 'the gateway to the Yangtze River, the wonderful East China Sea', it divides the Yangtze into two before it flows into the vast ocean.

The first time I crossed the Yangtze was in 1999, and the second time was in 2001 when I arrived at the source of the river. After reaching the estuary, I made a mental calculation of the number of times I had crossed the river: during the eight years of my journey, I had walked along the upper, middle and lower reaches of the river, crossing it a total of twenty-three times.

Just like the Yellow River, the Yangtze is also the mother river of China who has nurtured generations of Chinese sons and daughters for thousands of years. Unfortunately, no matter where humans live along the river, there is always man-made destruction and pollution. Every time I passed the river, I saw many riverside restaurants and local residents dump rubbish directly into the water. The discharge of industrial effluents along the river made the condition even worse. Sewage is often discharged into the river without any purification, seriously polluting the water. I was traumatised by this, as I had mistakenly drunk the contaminated water and suffered from vomiting and diarrhoea a few times.

Water is the source of life. The growth of everything on earth is linked to water. During these past few years, I formed a deeper understanding of the importance of water. On countless occasions I almost lost my life as a result of a lack of water. The hardest time was during droughts in unpopulated areas, where the only way I could survive was to drink my own blood or urine.

Perhaps most people take the accessibility of water for granted. Therefore, even when governments advocate water conservation, the phenomenon of wasting water can be seen everywhere. As a matter of fact, there are a plenty of places in China that face severe water shortages. If people can't see those places with their own eyes, it would be almost impossible for them to imagine the difficult lives led by others. In some places, people have to walk several miles to retrieve enough water to support the most basic needs of the family.

In the northwest, I witnessed the miserable condition of civilians in water-deficient areas. Many never bathe even once in their lifetime. Even on the most important day of their life, the wedding ceremony, people are only able to scrub their bodies out of courtesy. It is a source of pride to own a water cellar. In fact, even though some people possess water cellars, the water is often cloudy and can only be drunk after prolonged rainfall. In order to save more water, families have to share a single basin of water to wash their face and feet, and then pass on the water for their cattle and sheep to drink.

Air pollution

The results of serious deforestation

Slaughtered wild animals

A polluted river

Whenever I saw situations like this, I always felt sad and helpless, which was why I promoted environmental protection and water conservation to those I met on the way, hoping my efforts could make a small difference. I believe that if everyone starts from somewhere, the world will become a better place.

Big beer belly

On 14 May, I arrived at West Lake in Hangzhou. It was the second time that I had entered Zhejiang Province, seven years previously being the first. The legend of Xu Xian and White Snake, which has been told for thousands of years, adds some mystery and romance to the poetic and picturesque beauty of West Lake.

During peak tourist seasons, continuous streams of visitors come to the attraction. I walked around the lake and enjoyed the beautiful scenery as I was approaching Leifeng Tower. When passing through an open area, I saw a temporary stage surrounded by a huge crowd. Upon closer inspection, it turned out that Zhejiang Satellite TV was filming a beer contest event.

Thirsty and tired, I decided to take off my pack and rest while enjoying the show. The live performances were something to behold. One contestant drank beer through his nose and it seemed like he was seriously enjoying it; another opened a hundred bottles of beer with his teeth; a third contestant rode a bike on top of empty beer bottles fixed to the ground. What hidden talents!

Perhaps I looked different from those around me, since before I could even stretch my limbs, the host spotted me. He came up to me and asked: "We're going to invite ten people from the audience to compete in a beer-drinking competition with one of our professional contestants. Would you like to join us?"

"Why not!" I answered without thinking.

"Then let's welcome this brave friend," he said as he pulled me up to the stage.

The audience cheered, and whistles were blown from all corners. The host announced the rules of the two-part competition. The first part was 'who drinks the fastest', which involved finishing a bottle of beer within the shortest time. The second part was 'who drinks the most', which involved consuming the most beer within ten minutes. Contestants would get points corresponding to their rankings and the one who earned the most points would win.

"Go!" With a loud and clear order, the game began. Within a few mouthfuls, I had already finished the entire bottle. About a second later, the professional player finished too. As for the other contestants, some of them had drunk more than half, while others had managed to get their shirts wet without drinking very much at all. The host came to me, lifted my right hand and announced: "Congratulations! It only took you five seconds to finish the task. You are currently in first place."

Soon, we started the second part of the contest. In front of each contestant were six bottles of beer. With another loud call "Start now!", all the players began drinking. The live show was bustling with noise and excitement.

At the beer contest event

I glanced either side; everyone had finished their first bottle in approximately the same time; two players gave up on their second bottle; as I was drinking my third bottle, only three people were left on stage; when I raised my fourth bottle, only the professional player and I were left. The audience began to cheer wildly, waiting for the crucial moment of victory. The atmosphere was tense. Finishing half of the bottle, I saw that the professional player dropped his bottle and quit the game. It took me less than six minutes to finish four bottles of beer.

Having won both elements of the competition, I had the honour of receiving the 'Big Beer Belly' trophy. As I was accepting the award, the host asked me curiously: "Have you ever been in a beer competition before?"

"This is the first time," I answered.

"How come you can drink so much?"

"It's hot and I'm thirsty. Also, the beer is free!"

Before I could finish my answer, the audience was already laughing. Because I had drunk too much, too fast, beer foam started to flow out of my mouth. I began to feel unsteady and it felt as if my belly was about to burst.

Even though it was quite embarrassing to get drunk on stage, it was a fun experience. Before, in order to save money, I resisted buying even a single bottle of beer, let alone five bottles in one go. As a result, I enjoyed the competition regardless of my somewhat upset stomach.

This event was a brief interlude in my journey, an episode of joy amid hardship. Even now when I talk about it with friends, I still feel intrigued by it.

A love story

17 October 2006 was one of the darkest days of my life. On this day, with great pain in my heart, I ended my two-year relationship with the woman I deeply loved.

I first met Lin in April 2004. It was the second time I went to Yibin, Sichuan Province, the so-called land of abundance. A group of old friends had arranged a party for my arrival. It was during this party that I met the girl that would later leave a deep imprint on my life. She was there to meet me, the 'legendary man' as they called me.

Like a typical Sichuan girl, she was lively, cheerful and outgoing. Despite the fact that it was our first encounter, we soon found common interests and hobbies. When she was away from work, she liked to travel. So, when I told her my stories, she was fascinated by every detail. Before departing, she told me that she would love to have a chance to go hiking with me. I gladly agreed.

After I left Yibin, we began the habit of sending each other text messages. She told me that she remembered my promise to her and that she'd find an opportunity to travel with me.

A few months later, in July, I arrived in Yanqing District, Beijing. When Lin learned that I was in the capital, she decided to visit me. I thought she'd come with a few friends, so when she showed up alone, I was a little overwhelmed.

During the following five days, we walked along Guanting Reservoir, passed Kangxi Grassland, climbed the Great Wall and arrived in Tiananmen Square. We shared our interests, talked about family and friends, friendship and love, and dreamed about the future. Lin told me about her views on love; and I, too, explained to her my thoughts. I said that I didn't want to start a family until I had accomplished my dream.

Lin comes from a decent family. She's not only elegant and beautiful, but also very intelligent. During the long distances we walked together, her feet were rubbed raw and developed blisters; however, she never complained. When we were about to say goodbye, she said half-jokingly: "Lei, once you complete your journey, I will marry you!"

I replied in a similar fashion, "Lin, I will marry you once I realise my dream!" We both knew that we had already fallen in love with each other.

After we parted, our phone calls and text messages became increasingly frequent, and so did our care and longing for one another. Love is such a wonderful thing. When I first embarked on my journey, I warned myself not to start a relationship before I had reached my last destination. The truth was, when love came, it hit me like a flood, leaving me nowhere to hide. In the winter of 2005, I walked back to my home town to celebrate Chinese New Year with my family. Lin told me that she wanted to see the ice lantern festival in northeast China, but, most important, she wanted to see me. Regardless of her parents' objection, she came to my side. So naturally, as if arranged by God, we started a romantic relationship.

Lin was gentle and sensible. Whenever we spent time together, I was moved by how much she cared for me. During my later trips, my attachment to her grew with each passing day. Being able to share my thoughts and secrets with her made travelling alone more bearable and less lonely. Our love for each other also filled my heart with bliss. I had never had such a passionate affection for anyone before. Like all people in love, I felt like the happiest person in the world.

Over the course of two years, we transitioned from acquaintances to companions. We were more and more convinced that we were meant to be. But the cruel reality was that we were separate more often than we were together. Our yearning to see each other and the persistence of ideals caused problems in our relationship.

During the Mid-Autumn Festival, Lin said to me: "Lei, please stop walking. Let's start a company together, get married and have children. Have a normal life with me just like everyone else."

How I wish I could have stayed with the person I loved. But I couldn't just abandon a dream I'd pursued for so long. I still had two more years to go, and I wanted to walk through the holy land of my dreams, Lop Nur, the forbidden territory of life. Once I stepped in, I wouldn't know whether I could survive.

The unpredictability of my future led me to fall into a deep agony. After thinking things over, I decided to let go. If I couldn't give her the life she wanted, I had to leave so she could pursue a life without the burden of me. Nevertheless, my heart was filled with misery and reluctance.

This love, however painful it was at the end, left me with a beautiful memory that I would never forget. Love, like walking, is an exploration of life. The experience itself was a harvest and enjoyment. I never regretted falling in love with her.

Food poisoning

On 18 September, when I was walking in Wenzhou, Zhejiang Province, I was interviewed by a local newspaper, *Wenzhou Evening News*. A man, after seeing the news, found me in the Yadang Mountains after taking great trouble to track me down.

His name was Shaoyi. He told me that he always had a dream of travelling on foot from his home town Wenzhou to Hangzhou. But for various reasons, he was not able to fulfil his wish.

Shaoyi was regarded as a successful businessman. Due to a car accident a few years previously, one of his legs was permanently damaged. It was also because of that life-threatening accident that he started to have new insights into life. The idea of backpacking struck his mind.

A gentleman is always ready to help others attain their goals; moreover, it was hardly any trouble to have a companion on the road, so I gladly agreed to his request. To help him realise his dream sooner and to save me some time, I first told him about the preparations he needed to undertake before starting the trip with me.

On 10 December, when I reached Fujian Province, I received Shaoyi's phone call. He was ready. At that point, I put a stop to my original travel plan and took a bus to meet Shaoyi in Wenzhou.

When I arrived in Wenzhou the next day, Shaoyi had entered Yongjia County in Zhejiang Province, 28 kilometres from his home. Early next morning, we set off together in Yongjia County, and reached Lion Rock in Nanxi River Scenic Spot by night. A middle-aged woman walking on the side of the road approached us and invited us to her family-owned inn called Awai.

One night at the inn cost 145 yuan, and a meal was 120 yuan. It was only the first day and we had already spent so much. To someone who had been living on just a few yuan a day to sleep in a farmhouse or in his own tent, it was too extravagant. Seeing how uneasy I was, Shaoyi tried to reassure me: "Old Lei, now you are with me, just relax and enjoy!"

This Awai Inn was not just expensive. After dinner, we got ready for bed. Shortly after I laid down, my head began to ache violently, and my stomach was groaning. I checked my watch; it was 11pm. I moaned "Shaoyi!", and found that he too was tossing about on the bed. It turned out that he had gone to the bathroom three times already.

"I feel my head is going to split open. My stomach hurts so much. Please call a doctor." He could barely speak.

His symptoms were the same as mine. At first, I suspected carbon monoxide poisoning, but after a quick inspection, I eliminated that possibility. It was very likely to be food poisoning. I rushed to get the hostess and asked her to get a doctor.

She kept on muttering with impatience and eventually found us a vet.

When the vet looked at our symptoms, he immediately suggested we go to the hospital in Wenzhou.

Because of our remote location, it took us a while before we found a taxi, an unlicensed one. Since the unlicensed driver feared getting caught in the city, he dropped us off in Yongjia County. Then, we rushed to get another taxi towards downtown Wenzhou.

Shortly after we entered Wenzhou, our taxi was involved in an accident. As frustrated and exhausted as we were, we quickly changed to another car. Soon, I couldn't help but began to vomit again. The pungent smell almost made the driver gag, but he still drove us until we reached the hospital.

We were both diagnosed with food poisoning. Shaoyi's symptoms being worse, he got treated with intravenous medications; I was prescribed some medicine and told to rest on the bed.

His condition was much improved in the morning. We didn't want to stay at the hospital, so we found a hotel to stay at, where he received two more days of IV treatment. Afterwards, we went back to the Awai Inn to pack our bags.

As we were leaving the inn, we exchanged a look with each other. We both knew that we would never come back again.

Shaoyi struggled to recover from the illness as we continued on the trip. We ended up getting him more IV treatment in Yantou Town. He was trying to muster all his strength to overcome his illness. For someone who was so used to a leisurely life, such perseverance was very impressive.

As he was gradually recovering, we began to walk all day over hill and dale. We passed Xianju, Pan'an and Zhuji. On 26 December, we finally reached Hangzhou at 8pm. I took a few pictures of Shaoyi in front of the provincial government building, where we ended our fifteen-day trip.

Along the way, we forged a profound friendship. From then on, we began calling each other 'Dummy'. He often said that, despite not being understood nor getting paid, I still insisted on walking. For those reasons, I was a dummy. In 2008, before I entered Lop Nur, it was Shaoyi who cut off the long hair that I had been growing for ten years.

Looking back to my eight years of backpacking, the number of interviews, speeches and various social activities increased dramatically, as did the quality of life. Nonetheless, I felt more puzzled mentally. Compared with being confined by the ways of the world, the pure state of merging oneself with nature and the fearlessness of walking in the northwest desert were much more enjoyable.

When all was quiet at the dead of night, I began to clear my thoughts. Perhaps my next challenge was the search for inner peace, where I wouldn't get bewitched by human desires. Only then could I walk into Lop Nur without distraction and make it out alive, completing the final and most rewarding adventure of my backpacking experience.

I knew I could do it!

2007
THE LAST CHALLENGE

Throughout the years, I often encountered strangers who helped and supported me selflessly.

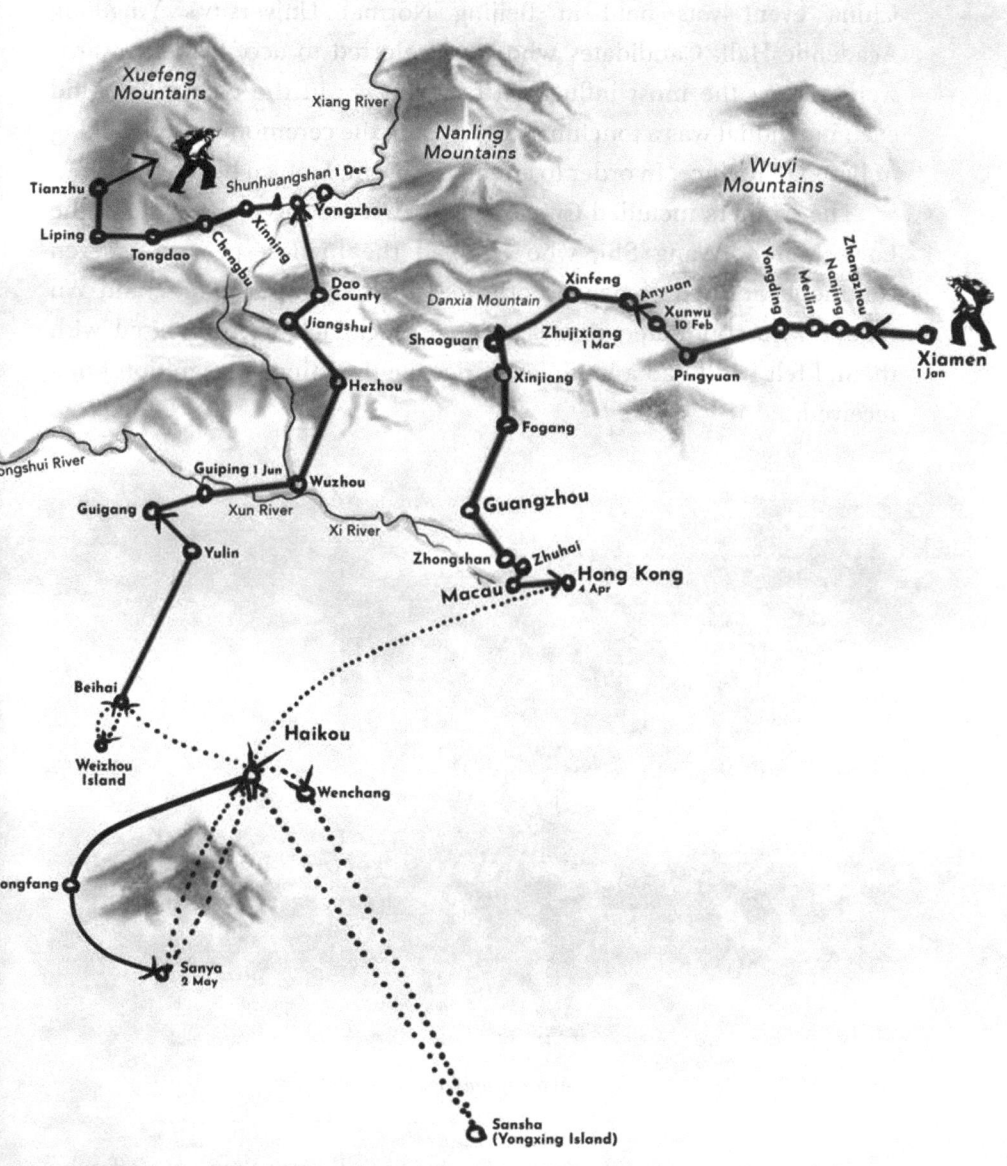

A pleasant surprise

On 3 February, the first awards ceremony of the Top Ten Backpackers in China event was held in Beijing Normal University's Yingdong Academic Hall. Candidates who were selected to accept their awards were among the most influential backpackers in the country. Behind each individual was a touching story. Before the ceremony, I was walking in Jiangxi Province. In order to attend the event, I took a bus to Beijing.

The winners included Cui Yongyuan, who retraced the route of the Long March, Wang Shi, who climbed the highest peaks on seven continents and who reached both the North and South Poles, and Wu Liqun, who conquered cancer through backpacking. Compared with them, I felt I still had a lot to learn, despite the minor recognition I had received.

At the awards ceremony

In fact, as early as July 2006, I received a call from the jury staff, who informed me that, after an extensive screening process, I had been chosen as an award candidate. To be considered for final selection, I had to prepare a record of my past achievements. I thought that, given the number of talented and experienced candidates, my chance of being selected was extremely low. Therefore, I didn't put much effort into preparing the material. Soon after I handed everything in, the event faded from my mind.

At the end of the year, a jury member called me again. This time, I was told that I had been selected as one of the top ten backpackers in China and that I was required to attend the awards ceremony on 3 February 2007 in Beijing. I was both astonished and thrilled upon hearing the news. I was surprised because backpacking had always been a personal goal; I wasn't expecting widespread attention or recognition from society. I was excited because it was a prestigious award and an acknowledgement that everything I had done was worth something.

Before the ceremony, I talked with a few of the other backpackers, many of whom I could relate to, giving me great comfort in an unfamiliar environment.

Cui Yongyuan, a famous CCTV host, led a team that made the *My Long March* TV programme to re-enact the Long March starting in Ruijin, Jiangsu Province. Through walking, he was also able to cure his chronic insomnia and depression caused by the strains of his job.

Wang Shi, a successful entrepreneur, found out he was critically ill at the age of fifty. Doctors advised him to be hospitalised or his illness could easily lead to paralysis. However he chose to take another path, one that involved challenging the limits of his body within the finite time that he had left. After successfully climbing the peaks of seven continents and reaching both the North and South Poles, he became one of the few explorers in the world to achieve the '7+2' goal.

Wu Liqun learned that she had got cancer shortly after retiring. Rather than allowing herself to be defeated by the disease, she decided to fight it through outdoor exercise. Following years of persistence in walking and hiking, her illness went into remission.

Their experiences inspired me hugely. Listening to their stories reaffirmed my belief that we are all part of mother nature, demonstrated by the positive effects that the outdoors and fresh air have on us.

The award was both satisfying and encouraging, and it provided the final incentive I needed to complete the rest of my journey.

My encounter with the post office

In March, during the beautiful spring season, I entered Guangdong Province for the second time. The last time I was there was in 1999. While I walked from east to west back then, this time I travelled from north to south.

On 12 March, I went to a post office in Xinjiang Town to post some letters and request a postmark to add to my notebook. This was normally an easy task; however, at this office, I received a stern refusal. Seeing that I was in danger of not getting a stamp, I hurried to explain my reasons. The woman refused to listen, nor did she bother to look at the documents I presented to her.

I asked her to contact her director, at which point she burst into a rage. She pointed to my head and yelled at the top of her lungs: "What? You want to talk to my director? Are you out of your mind? Get out of here! Or else I will call the police!"

She rushed out from behind the counter and started to jump up and down madly. She didn't stop cursing as she picked up the phone to call the police.

I've always been fond of post offices. Ever since the first day of my journey, I deposited all my savings into a postal savings account. Whether it was withdrawing money, posting parcels and letters, or making phone calls, the post office was the most convenient option. Not every place in China has a bank, but they all have a post office. To me, getting a postmark from every post office that I passed was essential, just like the monk Tang Xuanzang in *Journey to the West*, who had to get an official script and seal on his journey in order to get the scripture from the Western Heaven.

Although not all the post office staff I met understood my purpose, I had never encountered anyone so rude and unreasonable.

Little did I know that the police would come. Just a few minutes later, two police officers approached me ferociously.

"We need you to come with us to the police station."

At the police station, they opened my backpack and started examining everything that was in it. At the end, they came to the conclusion that my documents were fabricated and that they would be confiscated. I argued with them for at least an hour before other police officers arrived. They checked my documents and some recent newspaper stories, and finally they let me leave.

In all these years of walking, I encountered a myriad of dangerous situations; however, I found contempt and insult of my moral integrity to be the most unbearable. My mood could not have been grimmer. I knew, though, that having such a negative attitude would only impede the rest of my journey. I moved on and tried to channel this negative energy into forward momentum.

From 1998 to 2008, I collected more than seven thousand postmarks. I can proudly say that no one in China has collected more than me. Collecting seven thousand postmarks involved communicating with seven thousand postal workers. Some of them treated me with enthusiasm, some with care, some with apathy and some with torrents of abuse.

Every postmark was hard-earned, every postmark has a story, and every postmark was therefore extremely precious to me. Rain or shine, though hardship and danger, I gave them my utmost care and was able to keep every single one intact.

Heatstroke

In late April, after a gap of seven years, I returned to Haikou, Hainan Province.

The first time I arrived in Hainan was in March 2000, when I took the central route from Haikou to Tianya Haijiao via Wuzhi Mountain. I then walked northeast back to Haikou. This time, I decided to take a different route and walk west-bound and then south-bound to complete my dream of making a circuit of the Island.

On 18 April, I set off from Haikou, tramping over mountains and through ravines, and headed towards the city of Dongfang in western Hainan. The western part of Hainan is sparsely populated, with high mountains and dense forests. The road was rugged and the weather was hot and humid. The temperature reached 38 degrees Celsius when I was there. Every day, under the blazing sun, I trod on the earth with the utmost effort. Due to the high temperature and humidity, it was like being in a huge steamer. Breathing was very difficult and beads of sweat burned my eyes.

Due to chronic malnutrition and fatigue, coupled with high temperatures, my arms were swollen and I could barely make a fist. As I was walking at noon on 26 April, I suddenly felt a wave of dizziness and nausea. I knew it was heatstroke, so I quickly sat down in a shaded area and took some medicine.

Cold water would be so nice right now, I thought to myself.

Then, I spotted a bridge, under which was a ditch.

Thank God! I quickly ran over and washed my face in the water, but it was hot and only worsened my condition. Using my last bit of strength, I put down a layer of moisture-proof padding and laid down next to the ditch. I didn't know how much time passed, but I started to hallucinate, seeing myself pick up a bottle of iced water.

I slumbered until the following morning when I finally woke up. I rubbed my tired eyes and suddenly felt bursts of itchiness all over my body. I realised that my face, hands and entire body were all covered in mosquito bites. I could have easily been bitten to death that night, and that fear stung my heart.

After a few moments of grief, I continued my journey. From then on, I began taking herbal supplements every day to prevent a recurrence of heatstroke.

During my ten-year journey, I experienced heatstroke several times but was able to emerge safely out of danger every time.

In the summer of 1999, when I was walking in Jiangsu Province, I suffered from severe sunstroke and somehow fell into a deep sleep in the woods off the road. Fortunately, I was woken up by a local police officer who gave me some watermelon and water.

In the summer of 2000, I was travelling in Chongqing, one of China's three so-called 'furnaces'. Due to exhaustion and dehydration, I fainted on a rugged mountain road and eventually woke up in the heavy rain.

In the summer of 2003, while walking in the Turpan Depression in Xinjiang, the surface temperature reached 74 degrees Celsius. I got heatstroke several times a day. I had to rely on applying alcohol to my chest and back for relief.

Every time I thought about those moments when I kept on going despite the near-death experiences, I had a stronger belief in my dream. I thought, if I did my best, I would not regret pressing on even if I ultimately failed.

Woody Island

At 5pm on 11 May, at Qinglan Pier in Wenchang, Hainan Province, I boarded a supply ship called *Qiongsha No. 3* to the Paracel Islands in the South China Sea. It is usually difficult for an ordinary person to visit the islands; however, the naval base made an exception for me.

The ship bumped over the turbulent ocean waves the entire night before reaching the final destination the next morning, Woody Island. This is the largest of the Paracel Islands. Since it had just rained, the air was cool and fresh. A rainbow appeared in the sky, one end of it touching the ocean.

On shore, marines were already standing in line awaiting my arrival. Two of the young soldiers held up a sign saying 'Welcome Lei Diansheng'. I felt touched and honoured. Later, the general engineer at the military base arranged for my lodging and asked Shi, a young soldier, to show me around the island.

Due to high wind and a lack of soil, only a few types of plant can survive in this environment. Tall coconut trees grew throughout the island, but the most tenacious were the goat horn trees. Whenever a typhoon struck, branches fell to the ground but soon took root and quickly grew into new trees. Another type of tree called *kang feng tong* is similarly tenacious. On this island, I saw a primeval forest covering an area little greater than the size of a football pitch. It was said that the forest had existed for several centuries. The trunks were thick given the lack of soil on the island, the largest diameter reaching fifty centimetres.

There were more than a hundred fishermen living on Woody Island. Generations before them had also made a living from fishing. Since there was very little fresh water, the military and civilians depended on collecting rainwater and receiving water from a supply ship from Hainan. The soldiers told me that they initially felt very uncomfortable here, but they gradually got accustomed to it. What was more difficult than the lack of water was not being able to go home. Some soldiers had been on the island for two years. They often could not sleep at night from a yearning to see their families. Their main source of information came from satellite TV and phones.

Whenever we talked about the Olympic Games, the soldiers were all very enthusiastic and could go on and on. They heard that I had made a special flag for the Olympics, and they all asked for a photo with them standing in front of the flag. I was also lucky enough to get a postmark from the Paracel Islands.

Standing on Woody Island

I decided to leave after two days on the island because I didn't want to trouble the soldiers any longer. Once they heard that I was going, the younger marines all handed me letters they had written to their parents or lovers, entrusting me to take them to the mainland.

On 13 May, I again boarded *Qiongsha No. 3*. Once aboard, I saluted the soldiers. I would always remember them, who had devoted their youth and their energy to defend the peace of our country.

A secret recipe to repel snakes

On 28 November, I arrived in Yongzhou, Hunan Province, about to enter the 'snake district'. As I was walking, a line from an ancient story popped into my mind: "The country around Yongzhou is home to a curious snake with black skin and white spots. Any plant it touches dies." These words are from *Discourse of the Snake-Catcher* by Liu Zongyuan, a famous writer and poet who lived during the Tang dynasty.

The climate in the area between Yongzhou and Shunhuang Mountain National Forest Park in Dong'an is warm and moist, optimal for snakes. China has more than two hundred species of snakes, of which at least seventy inhabit Yongzhou. The sharp-nosed pit viper, coral snake, cobra, green bamboo snake and Mangshan pit viper are the most commonly seen venomous snakes in the area.

I gained a vast amount of experience regarding snakes during my years of hiking. Of all my countless encounters with snakes, one remains unforgettable.

In May 2000, I was walking in the Great Yao Mountain region in Guangxi Zhuang Autonomous Region, which is known for snakes. I often came across dozens or even hundreds of snakes in a single day. Sometimes I would step onto something soft and realise that it was a snake; other times a snake would quietly climb up and become entangled with my feet. I was also often caught off guard by snakes that dangled from trees like branches.

One day, I unwittingly stepped on a snake and my left leg was instantly bitten. The wound was extremely painful and black blood was soon oozing out. I instinctively knew that it was a poisonous snake. I hurried to take out a stethoscope and used it as a tourniquet to tighten the upper and lower area of my leg to prevent the venom from spreading further. With little time to think, I took out my knife and, without any anaesthesia, cut into my leg to remove the meat surrounding the wound till my bone was exposed.

At that moment, the excruciating pain was nothing in the face of survival. I forced as much blood out as possible by squeezing and sucking on my leg. I didn't stop until the blood turned bright red. I then disinfected and dressed the wound.

Fortunately, my strong physical condition allowed a fast recovery. To maximise my chances of survival, I began to research and experiment ways to repel snakes. At first, I tried using insecticide. Even though it was quite effective, it had side effects on the body. Later, I put together a recipe comprising realgar, red pepper, garlic powder, musk, nicotine and alcohol and made it into a portable potion.

This recipe worked wonders for me. I applied it on my shoes and trousers, and snakes would slither away after smelling it. I sprayed it on snakes directly, and they would instantaneously lose their senses.

With the help of this potion, I did not suffer any more snake attacks.

Amputation: The price I almost had to pay

Life is often accompanied by unforeseen risks. I managed to avoid snake attacks, but I couldn't escape the torment of disease. Because of my negligence, I almost paid a heavy price, amputation.

On 1 December, I arrived in Shunhuang Mountain National Forest Park. Because I was feeling uncomfortable from days of walking in wet conditions in a new pair of trainers, my feet became swollen and festered. Worse still, I caught a fever in the following days. Feeling sick and exhausted, I had to stop regularly to rest and to treat my wounds. As much as I hoped to recover soon, I knew these simple treatments could only temporarily alleviate the pain.

Later in the day, an off-road vehicle slowed down next to me. A few young men dressed in outdoor sportswear walked out and introduced themselves. They were impressed with my backpacking experience but were concerned about the injures to my feet.

At that time, I didn't have a comprehensive understanding of my injuries and naively regarded them as insignificant, yet painful wounds. So, when the young men offered to give me a ride to the clinic in town, I politely declined. They didn't try to persuade me further; instead, they gave me their numbers and told me to reach out to them once I arrived in Xinning.

For the next three days, they called me, constantly inquiring about my physical condition and reminding me to take care of my body. As I approached Xinning, they were already waiting for me outside the city.

A handsome young man came up to me and introduced himself as Doctor Li. He asked to check my foot injury. Because I had not taken a bath for a long time, I felt embarrassed to trouble him, so I declined his attempt to help and said that I was fine.

Ignoring my unwillingness to cooperate, he said to me sternly: "Mr Lei, listen to me. Your wound looks bad. You must let me check it, or else the consequences could be unimaginable."

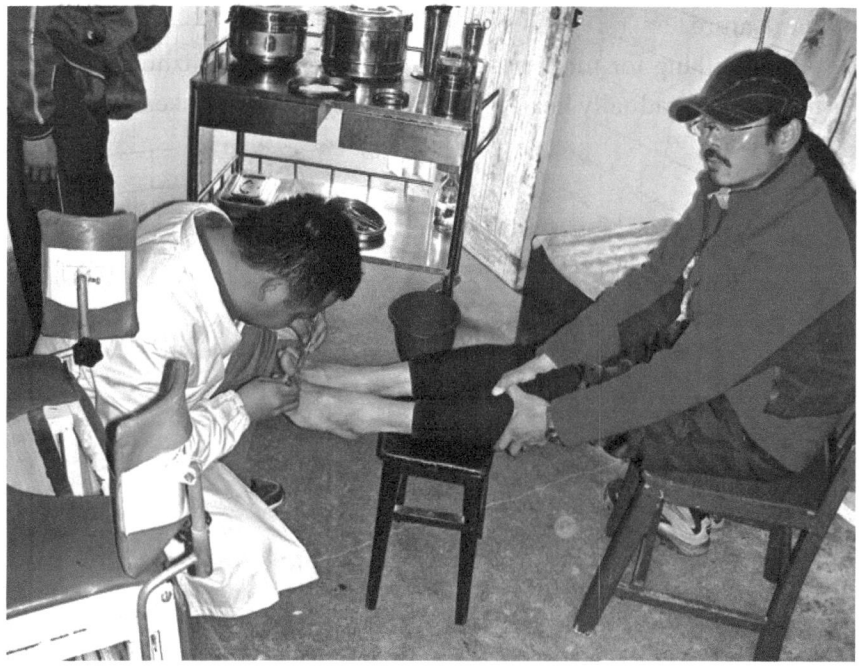

Receiving treatment at the hospital

I had to relent, so I sat down and took off my shoes and socks.

He was startled after a careful examination.

"Lei, your wounds have already festered. How have you managed to keep on walking? You must follow me to the hospital for treatment. I'm afraid that if you had waited any longer, you would have had to get an amputation."

I soon found myself travelling to the hospital with these kind men, still astounded. Once at the hospital, Dr Li disinfected my wounds and then use a scalpel to remove all the rotten parts of my feet. After about half an hour, he put medication on the wounds and bandaged my feet. Soon afterwards, I got an IV.

Thanks to Dr Li and his friends, my condition was under control.

Early in the morning on the third day, they set off firecrackers for me as a local custom for sending off relatives. At the point of departure, everyone was reluctant to let me go.

Throughout the years, I often encountered strangers who helped and supported me selflessly. Once again, I felt moved by the kindness of human nature.

After walking for more than ten days, I reached Guizhou Province. As my wound gradually healed, my footsteps became brisker.

2008
THE SONG OF LIFE

———

On the side of the road, I saw a plum tree standing proudly in the snow. A pink flower accented by yellow petals was frosted over with crystal clear ice, like an insect preserved in amber, creating a beautiful and eternal moment.

Perhaps my future life would take another form of walking; perhaps it would be another meditative journey.

Snowstorm

At the beginning of 2008, I encountered a snowstorm on a scale I had never seen before. I was on the border of Hunan and Hubei provinces.

At first, I was ecstatic to see snow blanket the earth. Surrounded by white, a few splashes of colour emerged in the landscape. Upon closer inspection, I saw that they were flowers standing tall in the roaring blizzard.

Beguiled by the beautiful scenery, I tried to take as many photos as possible. However, as the snow got heavier, houses and roadside petrol stations started to collapse. A winter wonderland soon turned into misery.

I continued to walk in the snowstorm silently and, without noticing it, arrived in the mountain area of Anhua County.

The surface of the road was as smooth as a mirror. I had to constantly change direction to avoid slipping. In the afternoon, as I was walking on the bank of the Zi River, a car suddenly skidded towards me. I tried to dodge out of the way, but I soon found myself also slipping down to the river below.

I was exhausted and the weight of my pack only accelerated my fall. Knowing that I would soon slide into the river, I desperately tried to find a rock and was finally able to cling onto one nearby. At that moment, my mind went blank and I reacted solely on survival instincts.

I first stabilised myself on the rock, then found a place to put my backpack on. I grabbed a rope, tied it to my backpack and held the other end.

I slowly inched myself up until I got to the road, at which point I pulled up my backpack. I collapsed on the ground, panting and my heart was beating ferociously. When I reached the vicinity of Wangcheng County, I saw a peculiar scene. The roadside electricity pylons were bent over from the weight of ice and snow, as if they were in low spirits. It turned out that the melted snow had turned into ice. And as more of it accumulated, the ice became as thick as glass. Despite their iron bones, the towers could not bear such a heavy load.

On the side of the road, I saw a plum tree standing proudly in the snow. A pink flower accented by yellow petals was frosted over with crystal clear ice, like an insect preserved in amber, creating a beautiful and eternal moment.

Seeing the flowers persevere in the face of mother nature, I myself could only hope to have the same strength as I continued my journey.

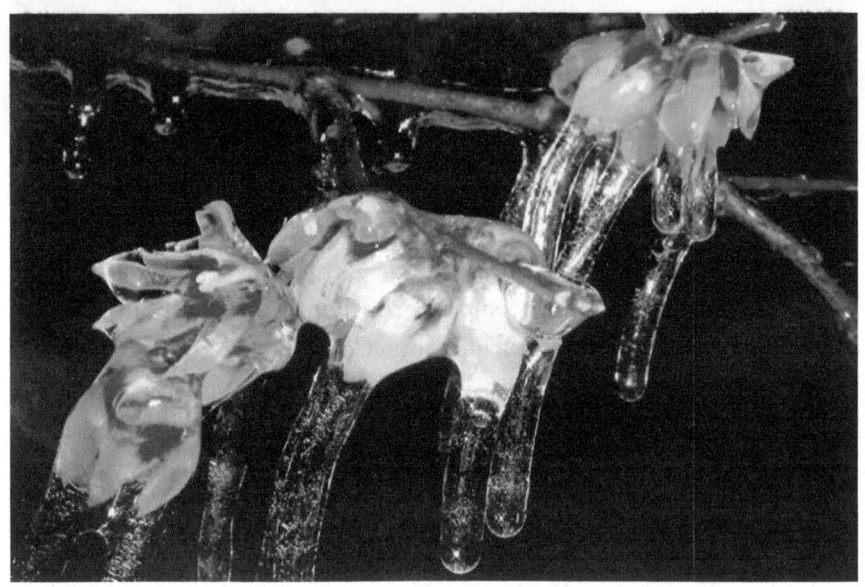

The plum tree covered in crustal clear ice

Drunk in Taiwan

In late March, I arrived in Xinzheng, Henan Province. After worshipping at the home town of the Yellow Emperor, I went up north to Anyang. It was then that I got the news that I had been granted an entry permit to Taiwan.

After years of effort, I became the first backpacker from the mainland to go to Taiwan, China's very own Treasure Island.

Early in the evening on 17 May, I arrived at Taiwan Taoyuan International Airport. On the second day, in the company of a few friends from Taiwan, I visited Alishan National Scenic Area, Sun Moon Lake and some other scenic spots.

I reached Kaohsiung on 20 May, the day when Ma Ying-Jeou took office. At night, an open-air concert was held at the Love River Plaza. Ma Ying-Jeou came from Taipei to attend. Huge crowds flocked to the brilliantly illuminated square. The splendour of the occasion surpassed anything I had seen before.

Late at night, I took a taxi back to the hotel. The driver didn't charge me a fare. "Compatriots on both sides of the straits are one family," he said. "It must not have been easy for you to travel from the mainland to Taiwan. I'll give you a free ride today."

These seemingly ordinary words were so heartwarming. In spite of the ideological difference and lack of communication between mainland China and Taiwan, the notion of sharing the same ancestor is rooted in the hearts of every Chinese person.

After Kaohsiung, I travelled to Kenting, Hualien City and then returned to Taipei. There, I visited the National Palace Museum, Dr Sun Yat-sen's Memorial Hall, the Taipei 101 skyscraper and a few other places.

Time flew by and the departure date was approaching. I felt content in having fulfilled my wish of travelling around the entire island and at the same time regretful that I was not able to travel by foot entirely due to various restrictions.

The night before my flight, Muqun, one of the friends who had accompanied me during the trip, held a farewell party for me. We ate authentic Taiwanese cuisine and drank 124-proof Golden Gate Kaoliang spirit. That night, we all chatted and drank to our hearts' content.

On the second day, when the plane took off and circled in the air, I looked back once more; I silently wished that next time, I could complete my wish to walk across Taiwan.

Becoming an Olympic torchbearer

On 3 July, I was on the border between Hebei and Tianjin when I received an important notice. I was required to go back to Harbin on 12 July to take part in the Olympic torch relay. I only knew later that I had already been selected as a torch bearer of the twenty-ninth Beijing Olympic Games on 26 February 2008.

After receiving the news, I was so excited that I couldn't sleep all night. I had never dreamed of such an honour.

There was not a speck of cloud in the sky on the morning of 12 July. At 8am, the torch relay began in front of the Harbin People Flood Control Success Memorial Tower. When the torch flame was passed on to me from the eighteenth torch bearer, I could barely restrain my excitement. Amid cheering from the crowd, I kissed the 'propitious cloud torch' and held it high.

Kissing the Olympic torch

It was a glorious route. I only wished that I could jog on a little longer. Soon, I passed the flame to the next person and stepped aside. When I arrived at the marshalling tent, my heart was pounding. I held the extinguished torch like treasure and I could still feel the lingering heat.

After the torch relay, I returned to my starting point and continued my journey. On 24 July, I passed Wuqing and Langfang, and then continued to Beijing alongside the Beijing-Tianjin intercity railway.

As the inauguration of the Olympics was approaching soon, the security measures were rigorous. When I was passing North China Oilfield, I got inspected four times by the police. At Anding Town Road in Beijing's Daxing District, I was stopped three times.

On 27 July, I went up north and passed Qingyundianzhen, Dahongmen Residential District, Donggaodi, Muxiyuan and Tianqiao. At dusk, I arrived at a hotel near the west gate of the Temple of Heaven.

This would probably be the last time I would stay at a hotel during my trek, because my next challenge was the boundless wilderness of Lop Nur. Just as I was thinking about haggling over the price of staying a night at the hotel, which was presumably very expensive given its location, the owner broke the silence.

"Look at you! You look like a chivalrous fellow!"

"Ha ha, I'm just a backpacker. How much does it cost to stay here for a night?"

"For you, it's free!"

I couldn't believe what I heard. Seeing the puzzled look on my face, the owner explained that he was a member of an auto club and that he also travelled frequently. He understood the difficulties that backpackers face. Therefore, the owner kindly offered me free accommodation and also bought me food.

Early the next morning, I left the hotel and went to the Temple of Heaven to worship and then arrived at Tiananmen Square, which marked the culmination of nine years, nine months and nine days of my journey. My next and final destination was Lop Nur, the sea of death.

Crossing Lop Nur

Lop Nur is a former salt lake located in the eastern part of the Tarim Basin. Previously, the lake occupied 5,350 square kilometres, but it dried up completely in 1972 due to the construction of dams that blocked the flow of water feeding into the lake system. I thought about crossing Lop Nur when I was walking in Korla, Xinjiang, in the autumn of 2002. However, local professional guides charged as much as 50,000 yuan and, more important, I didn't have a good knowledge of the terrain, landform or the level of difficulty I was about to face. Therefore, I decided to shelve the plan.

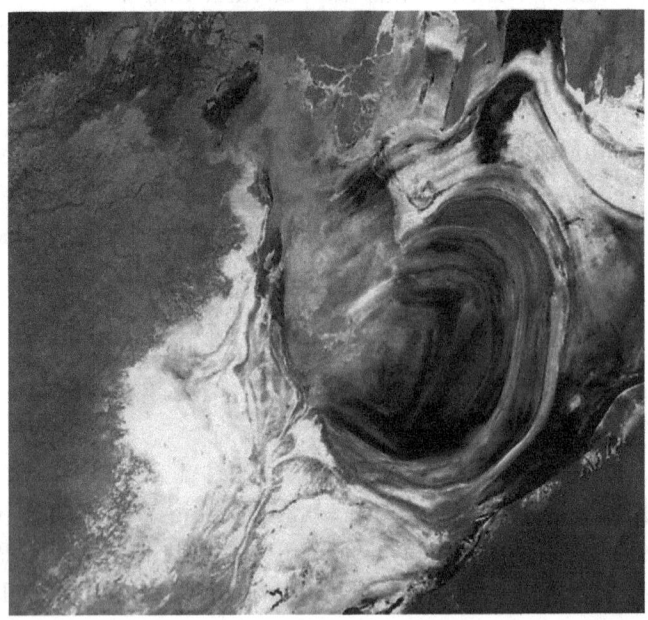

A satellite image of Lop Nur

Since then, walking across Lop Nur had always been a dream of mine. In order to fulfil this dream, I tried every means to save money and study as much as possible about Lop Nur. In August 2008, I returned to Harbin and began to make the final preparations.

West of Yangguan

Lop Nur is located in Ruoqiang County in the northeast of the Tarim Basin. In satellite images, it looks like a big ear laying across China's northwest frontier.

Seventy days after my arrival in Harbin, I was ready to enter this ear myself in order to understand this mysterious land. My plan was to cross Lop Nur from east to west.

I chose the ancient city ruins of Dunhuang, Gansu Province, as my place of departure, because of a poem by Wang Wei, a Tang dynasty poet.

> *No dust is raised on the road wet with morning rain,*
> *The willows by the hotel look so fresh and green.*
> *I invite you to drink one more cup of wine;*
> *West of Yangguan, old friends there'll be none.*

The artistic conception in this poem is deep and heroic. I wrote it down in my journal with mixed feelings, changing the last line to 'West of Yangguan is Lei Diansheng'. I made up my mind to cross Lop Nur, no matter what the outcome...

The night before departure was dark and terribly quiet. Only a few indistinct lights were blinking in the distance. Memories kept flashing in my mind, making it impossible for me to fall asleep. Weeks from now, would I walk out alive? Would I be able visit my parents' grave again?

Recoiling at the thought, I crawled up and took out my journal. I began writing a letter to my sister and brother-in-law.

This letter may be the last one I write in my life!

Dear sister and brother-in-law,

Greetings!
Ever since our parents passed away, your love and care for me have been more than what I could ask for. Especially during my ten-year journey, you have helped preserve an immense amount of information and material, so

that I could be free to focus on achieving the biggest dream of my life. Thank you for everything you have done for me.

This trip to Lop Nur has been a wish of mine for many years. Although I have drawn up a careful plan, I will still face unpredictable dangers. If I can't make it, please remember that I died chasing my dream and that you shouldn't feel sorry for me. If you hear news of my misfortune, don't come to Xinjiang. It's too far from Harbin. Ask my friends to bury me in the Lop Desert. This is a heaven devoid of any clamour. During holidays, please remember to pray for me.

In addition, please give all the materials I've collected throughout the years to responsible people who can sort them out and arrange for an exhibition. This would be the last wish of my life. I have 200,000 yuan in life insurance. Aside from the 30,000 yuan to return to my third brother, you should keep 30,000 yuan for yourselves. Donate the rest to the earthquake-stricken area in Sichuan for the construction of schools.

There are many contacts in my mobile phone and address book. If anything happens, please contact them.

Your little brother, Diansheng
8 October 2008, Dunhuang

On 9 October, I officially set off from Yangguan and headed northeast. I was accompanied by Liu Shaoyi and Luo Hongbin. In addition to a crowd of people seeing me off, an outside broadcast team from Heilongjiang TV was also there to report live. Before leaving, I lit three sticks of incense and drank spirits to worship heaven and earth, just like the ancient Chinese did before setting out on an expedition.

That night, we slept out in the Gobi Desert. The temperature during the daytime was around 35 degrees Celsius and would plunge to 1 degree Celsius before dawn. Early the next morning, I crawled out of the tent and climbed the nearby dunes to watch the red sun rising and to feel the vigour and desolation of the desert.

Passing through Yumen Pass and the ruins of the ancient Han Great Wall, we continued heading west. On 11 October, we reached the most western part of the yardang landform in Dunhuang, from which point we were considered to have entered the Lop Desert. Yardangs are elongated mounds and are commonly found in deserts. They are formed as a result of severe weathering that carve the bedrock into bizarre formations.

Yardang landforms

The turning point

The roads gradually faded from the horizon and a vast expanse of wasteland appeared in front of me.

Before heading in, I made an important decision, which was to ask Shaoyi to cut off the hair that I had been growing for the past ten years. Because, once I entered the desert, taking care of my hair would be troublesome; in addition, I was worried that I wouldn't come out alive. Leaving a part of me behind to the world could at least prove that I existed and that I fought for my dream.

"Dummy, do you really want me to cut your hair?" Shaoyi asked.

"Yes please, dummy," I replied

"I'm really going to cut your hair now?"

He hesitated one more time.

"Go ahead!"

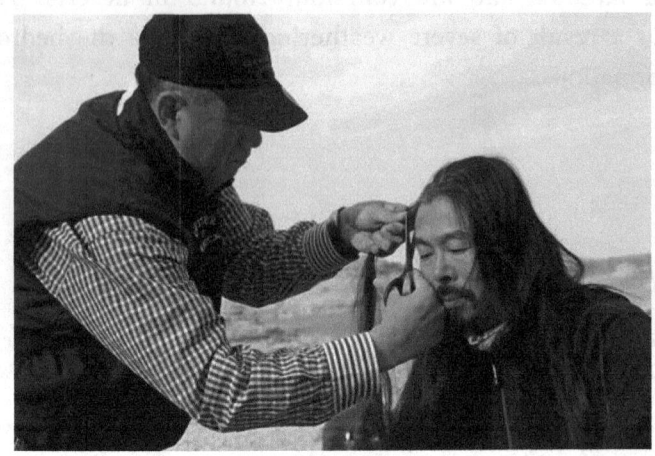

Cutting my hair

With a few snips of the scissors, the hair that had accompanied me through ten years of backpacking and the hair that had witnessed one challenge after another fell to the ground. At that moment, a multitude of feelings surged up. The oath that I wouldn't cut my hair until I finished my journey echoed in my ear. Today may be the end of my life, and it may also be a new beginning.

On the morning of the twelfth, a red banner printed with 'Lei Diansheng Send-off Celebration' was swaying in the wind in front of a yardang. Staff from Heilongjiang Television were busy preparing for a live broadcast. Multiple local press and television journalists were doing a live coverage of the event.

I was surprised to see many friends who had come to send me off. They treated me like their brother, giving me an amulet, biscuits, a solar charging board and a sentimental embrace. My heart was filled with gratitude.

A Mongolian man offered me some spirits, and I gulped down three bowls in one go. Then, a few Kazak girls performed beautiful folk dances full of ebullience.

Yuan came to me and placed a red cloth bag in my hand.

"Diansheng," she said, "this bag contains Buddhist relics. It's not a gift. Promise me that you will emerge and return it to me."

I understood her intention and put the bag in my inside pocket.

After I hugged everyone goodbye, I was on my way to the desert.

Before I had walked a few steps, some TV reporters caught up with me and told me that my elder sister was on the line. Overwhelmed with emotion, I didn't know how to even begin speaking with her. On the other end of the phone, my sister told me to be careful and that I had to make it home alive. Then she started sobbing uncontrollably, unable to say another word.

I held back my tears and hung up the phone. Without any further hesitation, I strode forward.

"Take care!" I heard the cries from behind. "Come back in one piece!"

That moment to me was deeply moving and was forever imprinted in my heart.

Their voices gradually faded. I looked back. Some of the people folded their hands in prayer, some were kneeling on the ground. Soon I would completely enter this no-man's land and disappear from sight.

Before leaving

I stood on a small sand dune and waved goodbye one last time. As I turned, the first tear broke free, and the rest followed in an unbroken stream. In front of me was a boundless desert, and I would be crossing it accompanied only by my strong belief in survival.

I walked quickly down the sand dune and wiped away the tears. Without looking back again, I continued northwest.

Sunrise in Lop Nur

In search of Peng Jiamu's relics

A few days later, I arrived at the foot of the Kuruktag Mountains. It is a mountain range without water or flora, with an average altitude of 1,109 metres. The mountains were a very rich grey, yellow, pink and white. It was as if I was walking in a carefully sketched painting. Fine sand particles covered the entire desolate land like a flowing blanket. For three days in a row, I roamed in this beautiful area.

Over the following days, I walked southwest towards Peng Jiamu's monument. At Heishankou, I saw a signpost constructed in 1969. One of the signs indicated that a left turn would take you to the place where Peng Jiamu went missing. The sky had already started to darken, so I decided to pitch tent nearby. Late at night, my tent began fluttering viciously in a gathering gale and fine sand was continuously being blown inside. I was soon woken up, feeling breathless. I had to wear the sleeping bag hood and a mask before I could sleep again.

By 11 October, I had been walking for nine days.

At 8.30am, the sun began to idle up from the horizon. I walked in an area between the desert and a belt of red willows. It was here that the famous scientist Peng Jiamu separated from his expedition team to look for water sources and eventually went missing. No one was able to find any trace of him since he disappeared on 17 June 1980.

The temperature started to rise as the sun climbed. It felt like walking on the edge of a stove. At noon the previous day, I found two bottles of water at a resupply point; however, I was already running out of water again and couldn't find another resupply point until today. The hot, dry weather made it difficult for me to walk at a brisk pace.

The humidity level in the Lop Desert is close to zero. Hence, large gasps can lead to substantial moisture loss. So, no matter how fatigued or hot I felt, I used only my nose to breathe.

In order to ensure that my remaining water supplies could last until the next day, I dug a sand pit to lie in at 3pm to reduce energy consumption during the hottest period of the day. Two hours later, I got up and continued walking.

At about 7pm, the sunset glow faded and the temperature soon plunged. Fortunately, I found Peng Jiamu's monument in time. It is located at 40 degrees, 12 minutes, 36.4 seconds North, 91 degrees, 53 minutes, 30.5 seconds East, at an attitude of about 767 metres.

Pitching tent next to Peng Jiamu's monument

The monument was erected in January 1982 by the Chinese Academy of Sciences and its Xinjiang branch. Travellers and researchers had paid tribute to the dead and left a mark of their visits with gifts and souvenirs placed next to the monument.

I pitched my tent next to the monument and planned to search for clues of his remains the next day. Unexpectedly, it began to drizzle. Tiny raindrops fell on the ground and rolled the sand into pieces of mud. Listening to the rain tap the tent, I began to have a curious feeling.

After about half an hour, the rain stopped and all was quiet, except for the low and steady sound of my heartbeat. Like lying in a vacuum, I sank deeply into my dreams.

At 8.30am, I set out in search of Jiamu's remains, but found nothing. When the sun was shining directly overhead, I felt like the Monkey King trapped in Taishang Laojun's alchemy stove, with nowhere to hide. Sweat trickled down my back, like condensation down a window pane. At about 2pm, the temperature reached 34 degrees Celsius and the sand under my feet was scorching. The stench of stale sweat that had seeped into my clothes for days attracted flies above my head. The endless buzzing sound almost drove me to the point of insanity. There was nothing I could do except to constantly wave my hands.

In the late afternoon, I returned to the monument and re-pitched my tent.

The next morning, Heilongjiang TV station made a second live broadcast. I performed a ceremonial toast in front of the monument and bowed deeply three times to worship the scientist who had devoted his life to the nation.

After the hour-long live broadcast, I started to feel a sharp pain in my feet. I took off my sand-filled-shoes and discovered that the blisters on my right foot were already infected, and that my left foot was covered in fungal patches. The pain was caused by sand getting into the wounds.

I was not yet reconciled to the fact that I hadn't found anything the previous day, so I continued my search in the direction of Tuya. I was told then by the support team that a lone wolf had been following me for 96 kilometres. Somehow the wolf had not yet attacked me.

The topography of Tuya is very complex. The outer range largely consists of fine sand, and, as I went further in, wind-eroded landforms occupied the area. To take bearings, I sometimes used a compass and other times used my judgment based on physical clues such as sand movement and certain geomorphic characteristics.

The landforms of Lop Nur

I slowed down my pace and carefully went through major areas of yardang, red willow belts, reed ponds and salt crust. Ever since Peng Jiamu's disappearance, many rescue and scientific teams went looking for him, but until today, no one has found any trace. I, too, was not able to discover anything.

As I continued searching, the temperature reached 40 degrees Celsius. I learned later that, when Jiamu was looking for water twenty-eight years ago, the surface temperature was as high as 70 degrees Celsius. The difficulty that he faced was indeed unimaginable.

Eventually, I decided to give up my search.

Horror by the grave of Yu Chunshun

At midnight on 26 October, I was woken up several times from the cold. I went outside to check the thermometer and it turned out to be minus 9 degrees Celsius. Thanks to the support staff from Heilongjiang TV station who had left some dry firewood on a road that I passed, I was able to start a fire and warm up some tinned congee.

At Yu Chunshun's grave

In the afternoon, I saw the monument marking the centre of Lop Nur. More than four hours later, I found myself standing in front of Yu Chunshun's grave, pondering. The preciousness of a relationship is being able to understand each other. Some people spend their lives together like strangers; others recall brief encounters with deep emotion. I only had the opportunity to meet Yu Chunshun once, in 1989; however, that fleeting moment forged a lasting friendship. I couldn't have imagined that, nineteen years later, our reunion would be separated by heaven and earth, life and death. I felt as if I could still see his kind smile and hear his thoughtful advice. Yu died in June 1996 when he was crossing Lop Nur. Today, I came to fulfil his long-cherished wish.

I placed a bottle of beer and a bottle of *baijiu* in front of his grave because he loved drinking. To cherish his memory, I decided to camp next to his grave and walk along the path he took from Tugen prior to his death.

At midnight, while I was asleep, I sensed a black handkerchief suddenly covering my mouth and I struggled to breathe. I frenziedly shook my head and let out a loud shriek. Sitting up, I found that the zip of the tent had been opened. I hastily zipped up the tent and took out my knife. My heart was beating violently and my body was covered in sweat.

I couldn't close my eyes until 3am. As soon as I was about to fall asleep, I heard a dismal noise from afar. It might have gone unnoticed, but in the deathly stillness of the wild, it was extremely clear. I was so frightened that my drowsiness instantly disappeared. For the entire night, there was not the slightest sound from outside except for the occasional strange noise. Clenching my knife, I remained in the same sitting posture until dawn. As soon as the sky started to lighten, I packed my bags and walked away from Yu Chunshun's grave, looking back every step of the way.

At noon, I reached a station that protects cultural relics dating from the ancient kingdom of Loulan, where I met three young men who were working there. I described to them what happened the previous night, and, to my surprise, they had heard something similar in the past but had not been able to identify the source.

Still bothered by the incident, I continued north and arrived at Tugen after 5pm. This area used to be an important traffic hub, granary and material supply base in western China. But now, it is a desolate place that only carries the silent memories of former times

Yu Chunshun had entered Lop Nur through Tugen. He fell to the ground at a fork in the road after walking for thirty-five kilometres and never stood up again. I had finally finished retracing his steps and the road that carried so many memories of him.

Walking in Lop Nur

Lost in a sandstorm

The morning of 22 October was extremely cold and my legs cramped several times from the chill. I was also running out of water and my satellite phone had died. Despite these setbacks, my goal remained of reaching the fourth campsite that day.

A sandstorm started to cover the sky, reducing visibility drastically. After walking for about five kilometres, I found a precious bottle of water buried by the support staff. It meant that I had not deviated from the route. However, for hours on end, I couldn't find another one.

At first, I thought that the staff had deliberately lengthened the distance between burial points; yet, twenty kilometres later, I still couldn't find any food or water. It was then that I started to wonder if I had gone the wrong way.

The road in front of me split into three. For a few seconds, I stood at the fork, unsure about which way to take. In the end, I chose the one on the left.

In the afternoon, the sun came out and shined without obstruction onto the desert. Left with just one bottle of water and half a bottle of urine, I had to reconsider how to stay alive if I couldn't find another supply point.

To prevent further loss of body fluids, I created a shade with my tent and clothes, under which I dug a hole and buried myself. Soon I started to feel drowsy. I didn't dare to fall asleep, because if I did, the sand pit could easily become my grave.

Later, as the sun finally began to set, I climbed out of the pit and started moving again. I decided to walk at night, because water evaporates much more slowly in lower temperatures.

The night was dark and quiet. Despite the loneliness and fear, there was only one thing on my mind: I must walk out alive. So, following the direction on the compass, I didn't stop walking until three hours later when I saw a coordinate tower.

I stood by the tower and lit some fireworks. Before long, lights and fireworks appeared from the southwest, a contact signal that I previously arranged with the support staff.

I desperately ran towards the light and at about 11pm, I finally reunited with the support staff at the campsite. When they hugged me, all my fear was swept away. That night, I told them about my experiences over the past fifty-one hours since losing contact.

Unfortunately, in the coming days, I once again lost contact with the base camp.

After waking up from the cold early on 5 November, I set out to search for wild Bactrian camels and the Xiaohe Cemetery, a burial site that contains about 330 tombs, the largest number of mummies in a single site ever found in the world

The Lop Desert is one of the last areas in the world that has wild Bactrian camels, a species that is critically endangered. I discovered some excrement, footprints and bones of the camel, and even encountered a Mongolian gazelle, some wild rabbits and a few other animals. I also found the carcass of a camel at dusk.

Wildlife in Lop Nur

Wildlife in Lop Nur

On the third day of losing contact, I spotted a few wolf footprints. Along with the fact that I only had half a bottle of water left, I started to become a little more anxious. In the afternoon, the hottest time of the day, I could no longer walk under the sun, so I laid down again in a sandpit. This time, I actually fell asleep. In my dream, a huge UFO landed in the Lop Desert, from which emerged a few tiny, oddly-shaped creatures that were walking towards me...

A gust of wind woke me up. The moisture in the pit made me a little chilly and I immediately stood up.

If I continued to search for the Xiaohe Cemetery, I would be risking my life. With no more water or food, I decided to change my route to look for the support staff.

At dusk, I saw the dried-out Kongque River. After walking west along the Kuruktag Mountain Range for hours on end, I finally saw lights in the distance. I quickly climbed up a tall sand dune and waved the flashlight frenziedly.

A few minutes later, car lights flashed in my direction, following which came the sound of an engine. After about half an hour, I saw the support staff. The first thing I said to them was "Water!" Then, I plumped down onto the ground.

After consuming two bottles of water and some food, I got up again and began walking towards the base camp. The car drove off and two people decided to walk with me. We were a little over twenty kilometres from the destination, and, at 2am, we finally arrived.

Lying in the tent, I looked back upon the three days of lost contact. I was still suffering from the shock of potentially losing my life. Even with just one navigational misjudgment, I may have never found my way back.

The final day

On the morning of 8 November, I began the final sprint.

When I was passing an old liquorice factory, I was surprised to find a man-made river. I hadn't seen such a clear river since I entered the Lop Desert. I immediately plunged in for a thorough wash.

At about 4pm, I arrived at the ruins of the ancient city of Yingpan, the finish line. In the distance, I could already make out a crowd of people who had come to see me.

Reaching the end of my journey

The flowers that they held seemed so vivid compared with the desolation of the desert.

After some short verbal exchanges, I could no longer control my emotions. I turned around and walked a few steps towards the desert. I fell on my knees and bowed down to this mysterious land that had allowed me to achieve my dream. Then, in the direction of my home town in the northeast, I touched my head to the ground three times to thank my parents for giving me life.

I burst into tears, tears that held ten years of memories and persistence.

Over the past thirty-one days, I had travelled more than 1,100 kilometres, realising my dream of walking across the Lop Desert. From the first day when I started my journey on 20 October 1998, it had been ten years and twenty days. I had left my footprints right across China. The feeling of accomplishment was indescribable. Hopefully this happiness might also have touched all those who had supported me and all those who were against me. Perhaps in realising what I had achieved, they themselves would seek out their own paths.

Life is like a song. I often found myself singing *On the Way*, a famous song performed by Liu Huan.

Life is a succession of lessons that must be lived to be understood. Perhaps my life from now on will take another form of walking; perhaps it will be another meditative journey.

AFTERWORD: ON THE ROAD

As I realised the dream of spending ten years travelling across China, as people learned that I had walked the longest distance, covered a route that went the furthest, visited fifty-six ethnic areas and became the first to successfully cross Lop Nur, the 'Sea of Death', I would inevitably be asked the same questions: Why travel on foot for ten years? What motivated you? How did you keep going to the end?

Overwhelmed by these questions, I often had difficulty answering them succinctly.

This decade-long journey involved lofty ambitions and deep discouragement; happiness and misery. I experienced the fear of death, yet also a sense of calmness having vanquished my own doubts. I was moved by kindness and love, and nursed grievances over cold-hearted discrimination.

This decade-long journey allowed me to witness the profundity of Chinese history, the magnificence of its landscapes, the joys and sorrows of life, the diversity of culture and ethnicity, and the spirituality of nature. All these experiences cleansed my soul like the waters of a clear mountain stream, ceaselessly enriching my life.

This decade-long journey gave me the opportunity to collect items that together weigh about two tons, to take forty thousand photos and to write down nearly a million words in my journal. I cannot tell exactly how many answers to life these collections can offer; all I can do is to share my story with the world.

The idea of becoming a backpacker took root in 1987, when China Post issued a set of stamps to commemorate the Ming dynasty traveller and geographer Xu Xiake. My resolve was reinforced by an encounter with Yu Chunshun, a contemporary backpacker, in the summer of 1989.

In order to achieve this dream, I embarked on ten years of physical and psychological preparation from 1989 to 1998. I consulted widely to establish a route, accumulated funds and spent a decade quietly preparing for my dream of walking across China.

Over these ten years, I planned to travel through every province, autonomous region, centrally-administered municipality, and the regions of Hong Kong, Macau and Taiwan; cross national border lines, coastlines, plateaus, canyons, forests, grasslands, deserts, gobis and no-man's land. I aimed to acquaint myself with local traditions and customs, examine the ecological environment and promote environmental awareness.

Between 1998 and 2008, the furthest points I reached were the Paracel Islands in the south, the Arctic Village in Mohe County, Heilongjiang Province in the north, Wusu Town, Fuyuan County, Heilongjiang Province in the east, and Jigen Village, Wuqia County, Xinjiang in the west. I have entered Tibet via six different routes, the Sichuan-Tibet, Yunnan-Tibet, Qinghai-Tibet, Sino-Nepalese and Xinjiang-Tibet highways, and National Highway 214. I spent a year travelling across the Qinghai-Tibet Plateau and another year travelling through Xinjiang. In ten years, I covered more than 81,000 kilometres.

Over the course of ten years, I lost nineteen toenails, wore out fifty-two pairs of shoes and developed two hundred blisters on my feet, including blood blisters. I was robbed nineteen times but beat the odds and survived. I encountered more than forty wild animals, and experienced mudslides, avalanches and tornadoes, narrowly avoiding death on numerous occasions. Out of hunger, I swallowed raw snake meat while exploring the Shennongjia Forest; I had to make a desperate escape from a python while exploring Luoxiao Mountain; I single-handedly fought off a pack of wolves as I was sheltering in the wild area of Ngari, Tibet; I drank my own blood and urine to survive while roaming the vast Gobi Desert.

I have met all kinds of people throughout the years. Some were supportive and some were hostile. In those difficult situations, I could only endure in silence. For the positive ones, I never took them for granted.

Ten years of backpacking has broadened my horizons. The constant collision of the fickleness of humans and the beauty and ruthlessness of mother nature has somehow allowed me to calm my inner self and has helped me to have a deeper understanding of the words of the Buddhist abbot Wanfeng: "Walking is like practising Buddhism."

Today, the joys and sorrows of the past decade remain clear and vivid before my eyes. I often recall those friends who selflessly helped me along the way and the amusing stories that have kept me smiling. Upon finishing this journey, I have again become all alone in this world. Yet my heart is full. I have found what I wanted the most. These experiences will forever be the most treasured and beautiful memories of my life.

The song *On the Road* by Liu Huan, which seemed to have been written specially for me, often echoed in my ears:

> That day, I had to be on the road,
> For the unabiding mind,
> For my self-esteem,
> For proving it.
> The traveller's sorrow is in my eyes.
> Frustration has turned into determination.
> On the road, the voices of my soul,
> On the road, for the companions in my life
> On the road, a distant journey of this life.
> On the road, for those who warm my heart,
> Those who warm my heart
> ……

Life is about pursuing one's dream. Striving to face choices and challenges is the only way to live without regrets. I have been very lucky to achieve my dream.

This book is dedicated to all those who have dreams or to those who want to dream; I hope my story finds you.

ABOUT THE AUTHOR

Lei Diansheng was born in 1963 in the far-northeastern city of Harbin. He endured a traumatic childhood due to the Cultural Revolution, losing his mother at age 13 and his father at age 15. His ten-year hike across China - inspired by a 1987 set of postage stamps commemorating the 17th century traveller Xu Xiake - covered 81,000 kilometres and made him the first person since the Tang Dynasty to attempt and complete a solo-crossing of the Lop Nur 'Sea of Death'. During the course of his journey he took more than 40,000 photographs, kept a travel journal of over one million words and rose to fame throughout China. In 2004 he entered the Guinness World Records, and in 2008 he helped to carry the torch for the Beijing Olympics.